About the Author

Despite his Welsh name, Gwilym Davies hails from Hampshire. His early interest in music making came in the skiffle craze of the sixties, strumming out chords on an old banjo. The folk music boom of the sixties awakened his curiosity to explore the roots of his folk culture which he then set out to research. As well as being a song collector, Gwilym is known as a singer and multi-instrumentalist musician and is an active performer in his locality. He has written many short publications on folk song, but this is his first venture into a longer work.

CATCH IT, BOTTLE IT AND PAINT IT
GREEN

Gwilym Davies

CATCH IT, BOTTLE IT AND PAINT IT GREEN

Vanguard Press

A CIP catalogue record for this title is
available from the British Library.
ISBN 978 1 784655 91 4

*Vanguard Press is an imprint of
Pegasus Elliot MacKenzie Publishers Ltd.
www.pegasuspublishers.com*

First Published in 2020

**Vanguard Press
Sheraton House Castle Park
Cambridge England**

Printed & Bound in Great Britain

Acknowledgements

There are many people I must thank. My wife Carol has accompanied me and supported me on many of my collecting trips. Mike Yates, with whom I collected songs in the late 1970s, was an inspiration to me in many ways. The late Paul Marsh similarly was a great help in my researching Hampshire songs. My Devon collecting was facilitated by my old friend Colin Andrews. Paul Burgess often accompanied me on my visits to Gypsy singers. In the USA, there are many people that I could thank, but especially George Ward and his late wife Vaughn, and the good folk of the Greater Washington Folklore Society.

But, mainly, I must thank all those folks who were kind enough to let me record them and who shared their music and good times with me.

Foreword

Anyone involved in traditional folk music – whether as researcher, listener or performer – owes a great deal to the 'collectors'. It is they who go out into the field and provide us with the evidence, the raw data, the repertoire, which we need to feed our interest and enthusiasm, and without them we would have nothing to be interested in.

The giants of the first wave of collecting activity in late Victorian and Edwardian times – Cecil Sharp, Ralph Vaughan Williams, Lucy Broadwood, and a select handful of others – bequeathed to us a huge amount of songs and tunes. Without their hard work, we would know almost nothing about the singing tastes and practices of previous generations of ordinary people, and an essential part of everyday cultural life would be lost to us. They worked mostly with pencil and paper – the only viable medium at the time for recording songs, although a few sound recordings from the time have survived.

After the Second World War, and the coming of the second Folk Revival of the 1960s, a new breed of collectors took to the field. This second wave had the distinct advantage of the motor car, and the tape recorder, and at last we could not just read the songs and tunes, but hear the voices of the singers, properly appreciate their style and skill, and get to know them as people.

But even with these technical advantages, folk song collecting still required considerable commitment of time, money, and expertise, and again, we who benefit from this work must be eternally grateful. This was all 'amateur', in the true sense of the word. Nobody paid them or supported their work – it was all done for love of the music, and the performers.

In the forefront of this new collecting effort were Gwilym and Carol Davies, who have amassed one of the most significant sound archives of the era. Much of their collection is already freely available on the wonderful Gloucestershire Traditions website (www. glostrad.com), and, as I write, the non-Gloucestershire material is being prepared for mounting on the British Library's online *Sounds* presentation, again free of charge.

Not content with making their recordings available to all, Gwilym and Carol are both breaking new ground in bringing their collected materials to a wider public. Carol's book *Really Beautiful Company* (Matador, 2017) is the first to be focused entirely on traditional singers and musicians, and with *Catch It, Bottle It and Paint It Green*, Gwilym turns the spotlight on himself, giving us the inside story, including his thoughts on the people and the material; but also, crucially, on the process of collecting. He is in an excellent position to do so.

It is in the nature of historical enquiry that, having pored over the material, we then start to get interested in the collectors themselves. Who were they? What drove them, and how did they go about their collecting? And, bringing in a potentially contentious topic, how did their own motives and prejudices influence the evidence they have bequeathed to us?

Apart from Cecil Sharp's fascinating diary of his American travels in 1916, we have little first-hand information about how the early collectors worked, and what made them tick. We must piece together a picture from letters, hints in newspaper accounts, and so on. We are in danger of being in the same situation with those who were active in the 1950s to the 1980s. That is why Gwilym's book is so important – as well as being a very interesting read.

Steve Roud
(a renowned writer, speaker, folklorist and librarian who has been researching British folklore for over thirty years.)

This is the Song

This is the song
This is the song of the farmer in the fields
Of the shepherd on the hills
Of the sower of seed
This is the song

This is the song of the Gypsy
Sitting by the campfire,
Listening to the songs of the older folk
This is the song

This is the song of the children in the playground
Skipping, clapping and dancing
To rhymes their grandparents knew
This is the song

This is the song of the soldier, sailor, airman
The ribald songs of the trenches,
Between watches or around the piano
This is the song

This is the song of the Christmas caroller,
Going from house to house with a cheery greeting
For a few coins
This is the song

This is the song of the mountain balladeer
With songs born in a far-off land and time
And passed on through generations
This is the song
This is their song
This is my song
This is our song.

Gwilym Davies 2018

Introduction

For the best part of five decades, I have been collecting folk songs and the occasional instrumental piece. By this, I don't mean writing out songs from books or CDs, or even obtaining songs from folk revivalists. No, my intention has been to go back further, to the singers and musicians that we call source singers – performers who carried the songs or tunes in their heads, with no (or minimal) reference to written or recorded media or to the folk revival. In the course of my searches I have found singers in Hampshire, where I started the collection, in Gloucestershire, where I have lived since the early 1970s, and wherever else I have found myself, including Devon and the USA. Doing this has given me a different perspective on what is tradition and what is a traditional performer.

When I started collecting songs in the early 1970s, it was still possible to go out of an evening and meet people (mostly men) whose memories stretched back to a previous century, with broad accents and even broader senses of humour, who had lived through two world wars, who grew up in the years before easy transport, telephones and mass media, at a time when the quickest way to get from A to B was by horse, and who made their living from the land. Many of them had seen the times when the only music they would have heard, apart from the odd scratchy 78rpm gramophone record, would have been self-generated, by the families themselves, by their companions, from the children in the street and from the odd village concert party. How different now, with piped music coming at us from all sides.

What I found in my collecting was different from the repertoire that the older collectors of the early twentieth century such as Cecil Sharp and Percy Grainger had found. Gone were most of the classic folk songs and ballads. Instead was a mixture of music-hall songs, drinking songs, comic songs, nonsense songs, rural ditties, and even bawdy songs. Rather than select what to record, I decided on a broad approach, trying to note the totality of what they sang and, especially in my later recordings, to note the provenance and context of the songs.

This book is not intended to be an academic work, but simply my various thoughts on English folk traditions. By the time it is published, it is hoped that the recordings themselves will be available to listen to on the British Library *Sounds* website, for free. The collection will be indexed by Place, Performer, and Title, and will be easy to navigate around. It comprises over 1,700 items and includes complete songs and tunes, as well as fragments and snatches of interviews. I estimate there to be about one thousand songs, and even allowing for duplication it probably amounts to over nine hundred distinct songs.

But the story does not end there. In recent years, when I have had any opportunity to record performances, I have preferred to use a camcorder, as this provides so much more information on the performer and his/her relationship with the song. These video recordings have not, to date, been deposited with the British Library Sound Archive, but still form part of my private collection.

My sincere hope is that my collection will be of use to performers and researchers for years to come. After I am gone, the collection will reside in the hands of my daughter in Cambridge.

Gwilym Davies
October 2020

Folk Song – But Not as We Know It

Picture the scene. Eight middle-aged but melodious folkies, including yours truly, have practised some local Gloucestershire Christmas carols with which to regale the good folks of Charlton Kings, on the edge of Cheltenham. After a successful tour around the houses of some friends, where we were greeted with mince pies and mulled wine, we eventually make our way in a rosy glow to the local pub. Now, Charlton Kings is really a big village; in fact, it was regarded as a separate village until about 1970, when it was subsumed into the town of Cheltenham. So, the pub customers are not trendy city types or students, but mainly good honest Gloucestershire working folk, many of whom frequent the local Working Men's Club (as it was once known). Confident that we will go down a storm in the pub, and that we are spreading a bit of local culture, we launch into 'The Holly and the Ivy'; not to the tune that everyone knows, you understand, but to an alternative nice, jolly Gloucestershire tune known to all the folkies but to very few other people. However, instead of the clientele being impressed with our scholarship and musicianship and hanging on to our every note, we are greeted with a chorus of 'Sing the proper tune!'. And we thought we *were* singing the 'proper tune'! We plough on to the end and then placate the by-now slightly alienated audience with a couple of better-known carols, at which point we decide to cut our losses, call it a day, and down a well-earned pint. At this stage, one of the locals, whose opinion I would not dare to question, mainly because he is about a foot taller than me, comes up and puts a firm but friendly arm around my shoulders and says, in broad Gloucestershire, but in the way that parents do when they are giving you some advice for your own good, 'You see, in this pub, we like the *traditional* carols.'

Now there's a thing. We thought we *were* singing the traditional carols, but the carols that we were singing, although collected in days of yore from the county of Gloucestershire, were not part of the cultural experience of the customers of that particular pub. Even though they were Gloucestershire carols, they weren't *their* carols, that they as a community knew and could identify with. So, we were both right about the tradition, but in different ways.

In the pages that follow, I want to delve further into this issue of tradition, and whose tradition is it anyway? Does your modern clubber with his or her mobile phone think of Cotswold Morris dancing as his 'tradition', or just something done by a group of eccentrics? Do the youth of today relate to, say, 'The Gloucestershire Wassail' as part of their tradition and heritage? When collectors of folk songs 'give' songs back to the people, are they unwanted gifts that go into the wastepaper bin of memory as soon as Christmas is over?

This modest volume recounts some of my experiences of collecting folk songs, but it also tries to show how the whole business of music-making is bound up with community and a feeling of common ownership and is not just another genre in the music industry. Although I have collected a good number of songs, some unique, others very common, I don't want to present just another book of folk songs. There are plenty of printed collections of folk songs and yet another would hardly make a ripple. No, this volume is meant to examine how traditions, especially in English folk song, have changed throughout the twentieth century, and how they are part of our culture in the twenty-first. Is folk music the new rock 'n' roll, or is rock 'n' roll simply the new folk music?

At the same time, I hope that this book will bring alive some of the amazing people that I have met and who have been kind enough, over the last forty years, to let me record their songs. The informants have ranged from illiterate Gypsies to cultured, Oxford-educated intellectuals, and from literally six to one hundred years old. They all have a tale to tell. I also want to give a flavour of the context in which these songs have been learned, performed, and cherished, be it the family circle, Saturday night at the pub, or in the playground. We have beneath our feet a huge vernacular culture which the media seems intent on ignoring and replacing with someone else's culture. Do we care? Should we care? Well, I think we should.

Let us start with a sweeping statement. We all know that society changes and that customs, habits, traditions, speech, and music all change also; but over the last century our English folklore has not been nurtured and supported. In the years between the wars when, for example, recording companies in the USA were scouring the American countryside for folk acts to record, no one was doing the equivalent in England. There must have been a huge amount of real folk music going on in the 1920s and 30s in English pubs, villages, and homes, but no real attempt was made to note it. The media, which at the time was just the BBC, was more intent on promoting classical music and jazz. English vernacular music just did not get a look in.

The English Folk Dance and Song Society (EFDSS) was equally culpable, perhaps more so, given that their remit was to promote English folk song and dance. It failed to grasp that the music collected by Cecil Sharp and others was music of the common people, but rather treated it as a pastime for the middle classes. There was a presumption that there was no more English folk music to collect, as Cecil Sharp had done it all. After Sharp's death in 1924, the Folk-Song Society and the English Folk Dance Society eventually merged to become, in 1932, the EFDSS. The Society was more concerned with promoting the songs and dances that Cecil Sharp had collected or researched, including seventeenth-century dances, rather than looking around to see what was still being performed and adding to the volume of information available. There was a disconnect between the activities of the EFDSS and what was going on in village communities.

The shortcomings of the EFDSS are brought into focus by the remarkable collecting of an American, James Madison Carpenter, who around 1930 toured the British Isles recording hours of ballads, wassails, folk songs, tunes, mummers' plays, and so on. His astonishing collection only came to light when the Library of Congress acquired it in the 1970s, and it has now been made available online through the Vaughan Williams Memorial Library Digital Archive. The fact that there was still a lot of English folk music going on which was ignored by the EFDSS was also shown up by the great volume of collecting carried out from the 1950s onwards by Peter Kennedy, who was working for the BBC, Russell Wortley, Mike Yates, John Howson, and many others. Think what we must have lost in terms of songs, tunes, and performances.

So, the EFDSS in the past did not do a good job of looking after our folk music. Happily, the EFDSS of today is much more of a forward-looking society, mindful of our folk heritage and striving to encourage and promote it and to involve younger audiences. It is making all the right noises – but is anyone out there actually listening? Is it still the unwanted Christmas gift?

Has society embraced English folk music? I think not, and it is still the preserve of a select group of individuals rather than a community affair (with some notable exceptions such as Padstow or Bampton-in-the-Bush).

But let us turn to the songs and music that I sought out, experienced, and collected. I have used the word 'collect' in connection with my folk-song recordings, but it is not a word I am at ease with. It implies picking up and taking away, which is not what I am trying to do. If I record a singer singing, say, 'All Jolly Fellows that Follow the Plough', I am not really 'collecting' that song, as it has already been found and noted many times in many different places already. No, what I am doing is recording the performance, the style and the context in which it was sung, the dialect or accent and variations in words or tune and noting the fact that the song was performed in a particular locality in a particular setting. When I started my collecting, I used a simple mono cassette recorder. In fact, it was not even mine, as I had borrowed it from my girlfriend of the time. However, technology has moved on and these days I am using an HD camcorder. With a visual record, one has much more information about how the singer presented and related to the song. The irony is that as recording technology improves, the number of source singers to record has diminished. How I would love to go back and re-record the singers I met in the 1970s and ask them more about themselves and their songs. However, surprisingly, I still occasionally find singers to record, even in the twenty-first century. Who said that the oral tradition is dead?

So, coming back to the word 'collect', although it is not an accurate word to describe the process, there have been times when it was appropriate. Some of the songs I have recorded have been noted for the first time, and some are rare gems in the oral tradition. For example, when I recorded 'The Schoolmaster's Son' from the Gypsy Danny Brazil, or the drinking song 'Mariners All' from Ray Driscoll, those songs had not been noted for many decades, and certainly never captured on tape. Similarly, when I recorded Charlie Clissold singing the tale of the 'Ledbury Clergyman', that was the first time that the song had been noted in full in the oral tradition. Song collecting can, in fact, be a little like antique collecting, the major difference being that you can put a cash value on an old painting or an old vase, but not on a piece of tape of an old song. How would you?

But to start at the very beginning (that's a very good place to start).

Roll Me Over

I would like to be able to say that I come from a long line of Hampshire traditional singers, but alas it is not true. The one bit of tradition that we do preserve in our family, and which we keep up to this day, is a first-footing custom, apparently passed on through my maternal grandmother, Granny Emily Faithfull from Hampshire. In this custom, the first person to step over the threshold after the New Year must be male and dark and he must carry a matchbox in which are three essential items, namely a piece of bread, a piece of coal, and a small silver coin. The matchbox must be kept in the kitchen drawer throughout the year. The symbolism is obvious, as the bread, coal, and coin will ensure food, warmth, and prosperity to the household for the following year.

There are a couple of drawbacks to the custom, the first being that coal is no longer available – you can't put gas-fired central heating into a matchbox. The other is that the first-footer needs to go outside the house at about five minutes to midnight on New Year's Eve and wait until after midnight to come in again. Many a New Year's Eve have I stood outside the door in the cold with my matchbox, hearing the peals of merriment, the chinking of glass, the 'Auld Lang Syne' and the New Year wishes, hugs, and kisses, and wondering whether I have been forgotten. To remedy this, I have embellished the custom by stating that, on entering, the first-footer should immediately be offered a glass of whisky. Although my hair is no longer as dark as it used to be, I have remedied that by wearing a black wig, so I am still the first-footer of the Davies family and no other volunteer has come forward. Funny that.

But as for songs, the only song that I learned from family tradition was at Christmas parties when my Auntie Jean would entertain the kids, namely myself and my many cousins, with hilarious games before bursting into:

Seats all round, seats all round,
Seats all round one penny
See the girl with the golden curl
And the gumboil on her… Seats all round, etc.,
etc.

And so on, repeating the lines over and over. This is not a song I have ever found in any of the great folk-song collections, or any collection, come to that. I wonder why. It was silly, but we kids loved to hear it and chant it with her.

My dear mother had many qualities, but musicality was not one of them, apart from, apparently, crooning

'Little man, you've had a busy day' to me when I was a baby. Mercifully, the song has not remained in my memory or repertoire. It is true that according to family tradition my grandfather Walter Bow, who was a thatcher from a Dorset village, played the concertina and sang in the pubs of rural Hampshire before and after the First World War, but as he died about twenty-four years before I was born, I didn't have an opportunity to learn songs at his knee. Walter used to play his concertina in the Red Lion in Southwick in Hampshire and never had to pay for a drink the whole evening. This is not an experience that has ever happened to me, despite having played many evenings in pubs! It was probably just as well that the locals were happy to buy my grandfather drinks, as I am sure he never had the money to buy them for himself. The only song that I know he sang, according to my aunts and uncles, was 'Fathom the Bowl', but to what tune is anyone's guess. However, in the 1970s I recorded a version from a family in nearby Petersfield, so I claim this as the family version – I know it is stretching a point, but that's the folk process for you. It would have been nice to have known Grandfather Bow, but at least I have a few family anecdotes and a couple of old photos, one posh one in a studio and one informal one, outside the Red Lion with a glass of beer in his hand.

Apart from that, the only singing we had at home in Portsmouth was when we sang along to *Sing Something Simple* on the BBC Light Programme, with the Cliff Adams Singers accompanied by the accordeon of Jack Emblow, bless him, or at the Saturday morning kids' cinema when we roared out 'Heart of my Heart' or 'Gilly Gilly Ossenfeffer Katzenellen Bogen by the Sea' while the words were projected on to the screen and someone played a glorious theatre organ which rose from the depths of the orchestra pit and changed colour every few minutes.

Our junior school teacher, the dear Mrs Lewis, with her hearing-aid and thumping piano, kept the class of forty-eight [*sic*!] eleven-year-olds under total control. Whilst drumming into us the fundamentals of long multiplication and parsing, she also taught us much about folk song and dance. Her teaching included several standard folk songs and it was from Mrs Lewis that I first learnt the Copper family song 'Twankydillo'. By the time I left junior school I knew a stack of songs, could get a tune out of a recorder, and knew how to dance various country dances, plus a sword dance. God bless Mrs Lewis.

However, my first encounter with 'real' folk song, although I did not realise it at the time, was thanks to the Portsmouth Northern Grammar School for Boys Combined Cadet Force in the early 1960s. The old soldiers' wartime repertoire had not been forgotten and our adolescent bawlings were, of course, true folk songs, but quite different from the ones that we learned from Mrs Lewis. Out of earshot of the teachers and in the back of army trucks, we sang:

The first time I met her, I met her in brown
All in brown, all in brown,
I pulled her knickers down
Down in the meadow so gay, so gay.

Very, very occasionally the song was clean, and we simply enjoyed its silliness. To the tune of 'Bless 'em All', we sang, repeatedly:

Goodbye horse, goodbye horse
I was saying goodbye to my horse
And as I was saying goodbye to my horse
I was saying goodbye to my horse.
Goodbye horse, etc.

Until someone shouted at us to shut up. Sometimes the song seemed to be clean but wasn't:

There once was a farmer who sat on a rick
A-ranting and raving and waving his…
Fist at some people who sat on his walls
A-teaching their children to play with their…
Bowstrings and arrows and weapons of war
When along came a lady, who looked like a…
Decent young woman who walked like a duck
Who said she'd invented a new way to…
Educate her children, to read and to write
While down in the cowsheds they were shovelling

the…
Contents of the cowshed from the back to the front
While the milkmaid was counting the hairs on
her…
Cows' fronts and cows' backs, that's the end of my
song
And if you think it's dirty, you're bloody well
wrong!

Not exactly Shakespeare.

So our journeys in the back of army lorries from camp to night exercise and back again to draughty barracks rang to the strains of such choice ditties as 'The Ball of Inverness', 'Three German Officers Crossed the Rhine', 'Roll Me Over in the Clover', 'Mobile', 'There Once Was a Farmer Who Sat on a Rick', and the epic saga of 'The Good Ship Venus'. In these songs, the fair heroines always had physical attributes of remarkable proportions, both above and below the waist, obliging natures, unending stamina, and libidos that would put bonobo monkeys to shame. The songs were rude, crude, non-PC, misogynist, sacrilegious, and, if the truth be known, great fun to sing. And they were true orally-transmitted folk songs. When we roared out –

Around her leg she wore a yellow garter
She wore it in the springtime and in the month of
May, hey, hey

And if you ask her why the hell she wears it
She wears it for that airman who is far, far away

– little did we imagine that, years from that date, Steeleye Span would have a hit with

All around my hat, I will wear a green willow
All around my hat for a twelvemonth and a day
And if anyone should ask me the reason why I'm
wearing it
It's all for my true love, who's far, far away.

Clearly the same song in essence, but our version had gone through the sensitive and imaginative minds and re-workings of Her Majesty's armed forces and generations of pubescent schoolboys.

A minor digression: it is a sad fact that there are few students of folk song interested in bawdy songs – a great pity, because these songs have lasted in many ways longer than the noble Child ballads. Moreover, I believe if you are going to study a subject such as folk tradition, you should study in its entirety and not just the bits that appeal to your sensitivities. Nor should anyone make value judgements as to the intrinsic worth of the material. After all, a doctor who is a GP does not choose to ignore the parts of the body that he/she is not interested in, but rather studies everything, both above and below the waist. By the same token, folklorists should study the oral transmission of bawdy songs. Of course, there is a time and a place for everything and I am not advocating singing bawdy songs at the family Christmas party, but in the right company…

When I was growing up, 'proper' folk song gradually dawned on us. In the mid- to late-1950s, the music world had moved on from the melodious but anodyne crooning of David Whitfield, Matt Monro, and Alma Cogan to the darker, more threatening sound of rock 'n' roll coming over to England in waves from the USA. I use the word 'threatening' advisedly, as the music industry, both here and in the USA, had until then been used to being in control and guiding people's tastes. Media music had been smooth, professional, and expressed safe values. Male singers and musicians wore lounge suits. Music was in the hands of the music business, and now suddenly the business realised that it was in danger of losing control over people's tastes. People were starting to decide for themselves what they liked, and it was rock 'n' roll. It is hard for today's youngsters to imagine what an impact rock 'n' roll had on society. The establishment was so enraged and shocked by the overt sexuality in the performance, rhythms, lyrics, and body language of Elvis Presley and other early rock 'n' roll singers that it literally shouted at them, 'Why are you doing this? What is wrong with the music we are already playing? Are you trying to corrupt the morals of our young people?' The truth was that such edginess, sexuality, and bluntness had already existed for years in, for instance, the underground world of vernacular music – folk music – but that wasn't the music that was reaching the airwaves or the record shops. Music was never the same again after Elvis.

In England, the effect was subtle and complex. Of course, the establishment was outraged by rock 'n' roll, but at the same time there were other influences on popular music coming from the other side of the pond. When Kenny Ball and his Jazzmen had a hit with 'Samantha', a song from the film *High Society*, played in New Orleans jazz style, the British public had literally never heard anything like it and were curious to know more. This one record set off the trad jazz craze in England and led people to discover and collect old 78s of Louis Armstrong and King Oliver, and to seek out both British and American musicians playing in the genre. Out of this scene came one man who more than any other was indirectly responsible for the folk revival in England. That man was Lonnie Donegan.

Lonnie was the banjo player in the excellent Chris Barber Jazz Band in the 1950s, and in the interval of their jazz sets, Lonnie and the rhythm section would play American blues and work songs, often to a furious percussive beat. And so skiffle was born. It was through skiffle that sections of the British public discovered that there were such things as blues and work songs and that they could be every bit as edgy, sexy, and anti-establishment as rock 'n' roll.

This is where I came in. I was persuaded by my mates to learn some chords on the ancient banjo I had inherited from my aunt, while they set about learning chords on cheap guitars. This, coupled with some enthusiastic but off-key harmonica playing, was the start of my musical career. It was raucous and not too musical, but we had great fun with it. Mercifully, our early attempts at skiffle were never inflicted on the public. But what we lacked in musicality we made up for in youthful enthusiasm. We sang whatever we came across, from 'On Top of Old Smokey' and 'The Blue-Tailed Fly' to 'I've Got My Mojo Working'. One thing led to another and before long we were learning songs from the records of Pete Seeger, Joan Baez, and Bob Dylan.

This was the point at which we started to realise that there was a world out there beyond what the media pushed at you, and that you were free to choose what you liked and disliked. As with rock 'n' roll, the songs of Bob Dylan caused a furore and once again the establishment, both political and musical, rose up in anger, accusing him of setting the youth of the day on the road to rebellion; which, of course, is exactly what he did. The fact that Dylan's songs dared to criticise politicians was more than they, the politicians, could bear. One cannot imagine a song of, say, Michael Holliday or the Cliff Adams Singers daring to say a word against the political policies of their day; but Dylan did, and the establishment couldn't take it.

Society changed forever in the late 1950s and 1960s. We felt the blasts of cultural and political air coming over from the USA, most of which we did not really understand, but which we parroted. That era that brought us rock 'n' roll also brought us the Civil Rights movement, the atom bomb, and the Cold War. America was the leading player in all this, but we were feeling the ripple effects.

In music, we all wanted to be American. This was not a new phenomenon, as even in the 1930s jazz had swept the country. But this time, in the 1950s and early 1960s, it was for real. We wanted to be Delta blues singers with the accent to match and a message to the world that it was good to be miserable and depressed and have the blues. We wanted to be Elvis Presley. We wanted to be Bob Dylan. We wanted to be Joan Baez. The sad thing is that, however good the British artists were, they could never be more than a pastiche of someone else's culture and there were few role models for us doing anything but Americana. Even today, you ain't got it in the pop world unless you can sound American – anything else sounds wrong to today's young listeners.

But what has all this to do with English folk music? The answer is that this interest in what we might call vernacular music, or music of the people by the people, led the British on a paper-chase that went from jazz to trad jazz and rhythm and blues to American popular folk singers, and thence to music from this side of the Atlantic, where we first discovered Irish and Scottish groups such as the Clancy Brothers with Tommy Makem, the Dubliners, and the Corries. It gradually dawned on those who spotted it that not everything had to be sung in an American accent. The Irish lilt was not our speech, but it sounded closer to home and made us realise for the first time that it was okay to sing in your own accent and opened the door to the possibility that even England or the English regions might have their own folk music.

So, where was *my* folk music? It wasn't the raucous Irish rebel songs, Delta blues, or Scottish mouth music. It must be there, but where?

The revelation came when my friend Tony Engle, a member of our first very amateur skiffle group, who later went on to run Topic Records, played me an LP of the Copper family from Rottingdean in Sussex. The Coppers had been quietly singing their family folk songs in Rottingdean for several centuries, usually in home-made, unaccompanied two-part harmony. Those in the know in the folk-song world were aware of them, but the folk revival was just beginning to discover them. When I heard them sing, on vinyl, my flabber couldn't have been more gasted. There were no gimmicks, guitars, or banjos; in fact, no accompaniment at all, and no attempt at an Irish, Scottish, or American accent. The singing was simple, but full, rich, and so natural that I felt that here at last were my musical roots. There were people singing folk songs in their natural southern English accent, so close to mine. Here was the answer, and I was annoyed that no one had told me about it before! Why had the media kept such music secret from me?

It has always been a source of curiosity to me when English people embrace, say, Mississippi blues or Irish songs as their own culture. Great music, of course, and fun to sing, but it is someone else's culture, not mine. When we sing those songs, it can never be more than pastiche.

Trips with Tony to Sussex to meet Bob Copper reinforced our bond with the music and to this day the Copper family are my all-time folk heroes. Tony and I were impoverished students in those days and a trip from Portsmouth to the other side of Brighton, a mere fifty miles, meant paying out money which we didn't have for a bus or train fare, so we hitch-hiked. When we tracked Bob Copper down in the Central Club at Peacehaven, he was more than happy to meet youngsters interested in his music and to sing us some of his family songs. We didn't even have a tape recorder, but he suggested that if on the following week we brought a tape along, he would record for us using his own tape recorder. Bob was a real gentleman, and very open and friendly with us. I can't see today's teenagers making the same trip.

Bob's contribution to English folk song has been enormous and for many decades he championed, in his quiet way, the essence of rural English song. It may be true that some of the Copper repertoire sounds a little twee these days, but songs like 'Claudy Banks', 'Adieu Sweet Lovely Nancy', 'Thousands or More', or 'Spencer the Rover' are constantly being rediscovered by converts to the world of folk song. The Coppers are equally loved, perhaps more so, on the east coast of America, where their concerts receive standing ovations. Although Bob in his lifetime was loved by the folk world, he was little known outside that circle. I could never understand why rich British pop stars were getting knighthoods (for services to...... themselves?) and Bob Copper only got a measly MBE, and that was when he only had a few months of his life to go. Why do we not treasure our tradition-bearers more?

The fact is that British, including English, folk music has never gone away. Throughout the 1950s the controversial visionary Peter Kennedy had been immersing himself in traditional music, song, and dance throughout the British Isles, recording singers and musicians from Shetland to the Channel Islands, and had presented various series of radio programmes, revolutionary for their time, where folk songs were sung by the actual singers whom Peter had recorded, rather than by 'trained' singers. His approach was at variance with the BBC policy at the time, where singers and musicians performing on the radio were expected to be professional artistes, not 'untrained' amateurs; but Peter stuck to his guns. The BBC worried that their listeners would not understand rural speech. However, the series of programmes, entitled *As I Roved Out* and mercilessly parodied by Peter Sellers on his recording *Suddenly It's Folk Song*, were worthy and ground-breaking and remembered with affection by some, but they did not impact on the psyche of most of the British public. Peter held his line on folk music throughout his long life until he died in 2006. He was a complex and sometimes infuriating personality, but he had the vision to see that what he was doing was helping to preserve and promulgate the real music of the people, rather than the music being promoted by the media. He was in many ways a man with flaws, particularly over vexing questions of ownership of the material, but he was a giant of a man in the folk-music movement whose contribution has yet to be fully assessed and valued.

Although Peter was from a family deeply immersed in the activities of the EFDSS, he did not meekly follow their policies and became a nagging thorn in their side through advocating that more attention be given to the real folk performers, rather than concentrating on the historical legacy of the great Cecil Sharp. So far as most of the EFDSS was concerned, both before and after the Second World War, Sharp's legacy mainly consisted of his revival of seventeenth-century courtly dances, beloved of lady schoolteachers, but having nothing to do with the real world of vernacular culture. In fact, the EFDSS, while claiming to encourage the music of the people, did not go to the people to ascertain what music was still being performed in village communities. It is undeniable that the EFDSS failed to capitalise on Sharp's great collecting work – so far as they were concerned, all the songs had been collected and there were no more to find. Nor did they encourage vernacular performers any more than the BBC did: folk songs and dances were fine so long as they were performed by 'proper' singers and musicians.

Kennedy himself, on moving to Northumbria in the late 1940s as the area representative for the EFDSS, was amazed to find an active living tradition of song, dance, and music, which the Society knew nothing about. The country dances Peter was collecting were all very well, but the EFDSS showed no particular interest. It is sad to recount that remnants of this attitude remained right through to the 1970s, when the band dance style beloved of the EFDSS was largely based on American or Scottish folk dance music, at the very time when expert traditional melodeon and concertina players such as Bob Cann in Devon, Scan Tester in Sussex, and Oscar Woods in Suffolk, not to mention a whole galaxy of Northumbrian musicians, were being discovered by the folk revival.

Be I 'Ampshire

Having come through the folk revival of the 1960s, I became increasingly interested in the notion that there must be more traditional songs out there to collect, and that there was possibly a sub-culture beneath my feet that I ought to find out about. The folk club scene at that time was great fun; there was a buzz about it and it led to some iconic performers and performances. However, for all the euphoria about folk song in that decade, I still felt that it was something that people did as an exclusive hobby, outside 'real' society, whatever that was. Also, the folk revival was creating its own style, which was a mixture of Irish, Scottish, and American influences. As I have already said, Tony and I meeting the Copper family was a Road to Damascus moment. Until that point, my broad Hampshire and Tony's Portsmouth accent did not do it for the folk club scene. This may seem blindingly obvious now but wasn't then when you had to sound like Joan Baez, Bob Dylan, or the Clancy Brothers. Tony and I never sounded remotely like Joan Baez, in style or accent, so that was okay; but we did learn and perform a great number of her songs in the local folk clubs.

With these barely-digested and half-processed

ideas running through my brain, I embarked in the early 1970s on my first real attempt at folk-song collecting in Hampshire, around the Basingstoke area, where I lived and worked for a couple of years. Looking back, what I was attempting to do was to 'discover' local folk songs, and in doing so to discover my own roots. Also, looking back on it, I did everything wrong. I used an inexpensive, borrowed mono cassette recorder, I didn't 'set up' the recording acoustics, and I didn't ask the singers about their backgrounds or how they learned the songs. So, my recordings of those days are full of background noise, the clattering of one-armed bandits, missed starts, and so on. I did manage to find and record several old singers but got so excited about finding them that I failed to note the background and context. Nevertheless, I feel that the recordings I made in those days still have value for today's researchers and singers.

My first efforts were to make some notes on local traditions. Bill Yalden of Long Sutton, a small village near Basingstoke, told me that they used to go 'wassailing', with blackened faces, singing carols from door to door. Bill would have been born around 1900, so presumably this activity would have been just before or just after the First World War. This wassailing seems to have been different from the West Country version, as he did not mention any particular song connected with the custom. Bill also described to me village musicians dressed in smocks, with tambourine, banjo, and triangle. It is worth noting that the surname Yalden is very localised to Hampshire and rare elsewhere, and that the Yaldens go back many years in that locality.

Bill took me to meet an old friend of his in a retirement home in Basingstoke, namely Charlie Milam, born in about 1880. Charlie was from Long Sutton and had been a carter all his life. It was thrilling for me to hear Charlie sing to me his versions of 'John Barleycorn' and 'While Gamekeepers Lie Sleeping'. My excitement at hearing the songs totally drove out all thoughts of further background research into how, where, and why he learned the songs, questions I would certainly put to a singer these days. Charlie had a gentle way of putting a song across but struggled to remember some of the words. I only visited him the once, which was a shame, as he died shortly afterwards.

Similarly, when in 1970 I recorded Arthur Baker, a bright eighty-four-year-old, who at the age of thirteen had been tending sheep in the Hampshire countryside, I felt that I was capturing a bit of old England. Arthur had a large repertoire of songs, mainly of the sentimental music-hall type, but sang every Sunday in the Fox public house at Upton Grey, encouraged by his son and daughter-in-law. He was usually insistent on singing a song all the way through, and always 'performed' the song. He also reinforced for me the notion that the folk repertoire is not all about old folk songs; and songs such as 'Break the News to Mother' and 'Goodbye My Bluebell' (both American songs, incidentally) had the same value in Arthur's singing as 'All Jolly Fellows that Follow the Plough' or 'Jim the Carter's Lad'.

Singers' perceptions of songs can be surprising. On one occasion, having recorded Arthur singing 'The Young Sailor Cut Down in his Prime', a tuneful ditty about a jolly jack tar who succumbs to a sexually transmitted disease, he turned to me and said, 'Don't sing that song in Portsmouth, boy, 'cos they don't like to hear it down there. You know what he died of, don't you, *the clap*!' For Arthur, the idea of singing the song in a city with a centuries-old naval tradition was beyond the pale, and I can honestly say that I have never sung it in Portsmouth and would hesitate to do so, lest I get set upon by angry matelots.

Arthur was a lovely old chap and one of the first real source singers that I met and recorded. From time to time he would come out with a rare song with roots in old English erotic imagery:

It's through a shooting gallery I'm settled now for life
For there I first beheld the girl I since had made my wife
She held my rifle in her hand in such a winning way
And when I took it from her, she smilingly did say
'You've got to hit the bull's-eye before you ring

.

45

the bell
Take a steady aim, love, and try to do it well
Hold your rifle higher and don't let it misfire
For you've got to hit the bull's-eye before you ring
the bell.

Well, ding, ding, dong, I say. Arthur sang that song with a twinkle in his eye and a chuckle in his voice. Who knows what erotic episodes of his youth he was reliving in his mind!

From time to time my collecting efforts led to frustration. I remember meeting a couple of old locals in a Hampshire churchyard who looked for the entire world as though they would be full of songs. Having greeted them, I swiftly moved the subject on to old songs, like you do, and my heart skipped when they replied, 'You mean, like "What's the Life of a Man" or "Once I was a Merry Ploughboy"?'

'That's the sort of thing,' I said, thinking I was on to a winner here.

Only for them to respond, 'No, sorry, we don't know any of those songs.' Ah well, close but not close enough.

My early efforts at collecting impressed upon me that, so far as the old singers were concerned, there was nothing sacred or precious about what I was calling a folk song. A song was a song, and you either sang it or you didn't. On one occasion I went with Tony Engle and friends to visit old Turp Brown in Cheriton,

Hampshire. Victor 'Turp' Brown was a regular at the H H Inn in Cheriton, the pub where Bob Copper was once the landlord. One of his songs was 'Six Jolly Miners', which the folk-song collector George Gardiner had noted many years previously from Turp's father. Bob Copper noted several songs from Turp, including the beautiful and mysterious 'Streams of Lovely Nancy'. Naturally we asked him to sing and he launched into 'Back Home in Tennessee'. My first reaction was shock. Why would he choose to sing an American pop song of the early twentieth century rather than an old English folk song? I thought he was winding us up; but no, that song was part of his repertoire just as much as the old folk songs that Bob had collected from him. Revival singers are often selective and might just concentrate on, say, sea shanties or long ballads, whereas the traditional singer will sing anything that appeals and comes his/her way, without making a value judgement as to the worthiness of the song. One old singer I recorded, Jack Oakley, told me that his favourite songs were 'Henry Morton' (a version of the old ballad 'Henry Martin'), 'The Farmer's Boy', and 'A Four-Legged Friend'. So, a centuries-old ballad, a nineteenth-century sentimental song, and a recent cowboy song all found equal favour in his eyes. But let me tell you more of Jack and his family.

On one occasion in the early 1970s, my Hampshire friends and I, acting on a tip-off, made a trip to a nearby pub, where we were told we would find an old singer. The pub, the Harrow Inn in Steep, in deepest Hampshire, outside Petersfield, was and still is a delight. It is an old pub with two rustic bars, wooden tables, beer straight from the barrel, dried hops over the bar, and a selection of books and magazines for you to read while you sip your ale. Their home-made soup is legendary and very filling. Going into the bar was literally like stepping back in time, and when we were met by the local character, old Jack Oakley, sporting impressive side whiskers and wearing plus fours and a hacking jacket, we knew that we had found the right man. It did not take long to get him singing and he went through his repertoire of 'Fathom the Bowl', 'Henry Morton', and 'Box on her Head'. He even knew a snatch of what he called 'Islington Fair', a Hampshire version of 'Widecombe Fair'. Unfortunately, Jack was well past his singing prime at that time and not in the best of health, so the tunes wavered considerably.

My wife, Carol, and I returned to the pub a few days later and got talking to the landlady, Eileen McCutcheon, who happened to be Jack's niece. Eileen sympathised with us that we had not been able to get the tunes accurately, and after a while she said, 'Well, why not ask Jack's sister?' On enquiring where Jack's sister was, we were informed that she was in the back room of the pub. We were duly ushered in and met the delightful Annie May Dodd, a lady roughly the shape of a cottage loaf, who greeted us warmly. She proceeded not only to sing us, in tune, all of Jack's songs, but added some more to the tally. We even collected a song by telephone when she suggested that we ring her son John Dodd, who sang down the phone to us.

Annie May Dodd of the Harrow Inn,
Sleep, Hampshire in about 1970
Photo courtesy of the Harrow Inn.

At this point it is worth filling out the picture. You will probably have seen West Country postcards showing a local character clutching a pint and giving us 'Greetin's vrum Dear ol' Deb'n', followed by a dialect rhyme. If you delve deeper into the subject, you will find the same photo of the same worthy inviting you to come to 'Dear ol' Darzet', or 'Dear ol' Zummerzet'. The rustic worthy is, of course, old Jack Oakley. Jack was a retired gamekeeper who lived most of his life in Hampshire. His photo was snapped by a passing freelance photographer who sold it to a postcard company. Jack, of course, never got a penny for the photo, and so his family decided that if he was going to play the part of the archetypal English rustic, then he would jolly well look the part. They proceeded to purchase for him an old-fashioned gamekeeper's jacket and breeches, a smart waistcoat, and a feathered hat. He became a permanent fixture in the bar of the Harrow Inn and regaled many a passing tourist with tales of old England in return for a pint – not to mention being the judge of the annual 'lovely legs' competition. When he passed away in 1973, the world became a duller place.

At times, the folk revival can be so inward-looking that it overlooks the living tradition under its nose. Eileen McCutcheon told me that the pub often had visiting Morris dancers, who, as they do, ended their evening's performance with a singaround. Eileen, on hearing their version of 'Fathom the Bowl', learned from a recording of the Watersons, dared to tell them that they had got the tune wrong; only to be told no, they hadn't. Now, with my folk-song collector's hat on, if someone says to me, 'That's not the right tune', I would reply, 'Well, how does *your* tune go, then?' Thus, the biodiversity of the tradition is kept going.

Ere's greetens vrom DARZET

Ave 'ee bin on Darzet cliff tops
Looked on luvly coves below
Watched tha zhips vrom other waters
Buzy goin' to an' vro

Rugged beaches, caves an' inlets
Girt arched rock ov Durdle Door
Meakes 'ee think ov many a zmuggler
Luggin' loot up on tha zhore

Nowadaays tiz lobster-catchin'
'Do 'ee vancy oone vor tea?

Greetins vrum dere ol' Deb'n

Yurs a welcum vrum dere ol' Deb'n
    The zunnest place this zide o' Heaven—
Vull o' 'istory, an' claims tu vame—
    With "Scrumpy", "Dumblins"
                an' "Clotted Crame"

Quaint thatched cottages, an' vields
                zo green—
    The purtiest scenery yu've ever zeen
The wild, rolling Moors, zo majestic
                an' grand—
    Wi' deep-wooded valleys, an' zea
                close at 'and.

In Deb'n the fust thing the local volks zay

Greetins vrum Zummerzet

Zummerzet greets thee wi' a smile—
    With "Welcum" offered ev'ry mile—
There's zo many things vur thee tu zee—
    Yu'll wunder zometimes, where yu be.

The 'andsome churches, wi' girt 'igh
                towers—
    Picturesque valleys, zo purty wi'
                vlowers—
The grandeur o' Cheddar, wi' cliffs
                zo sheer—
    Iz zummat yu'll never ferget, m'dear.

The Roman remains at Bath must
                be zeen—
    Yu can "take the waters" if yu be
                zo keen !—
Yurs greetins to thee vrum Zummerzet—
    A bootiful county, yu'll never ferget.

*Jack Oakley of Steep, Hampshire. Despite the postcards, he spent
most of his life in Hampshire.*

51

Encounters with singers such as Charlie Milam, Arthur Baker, Jack Oakley, and Annie May Dodd reinforced my feeling that I was at last discovering the latent culture of my home county. The one occasion that sealed it for me was when I met the almost legendary George Privett in Sam's Hotel, Shedfield, outside Portsmouth. I had been recommended to go to Sam's by the folklorist Rollo Woods, who made a quiet but considerable contribution towards folk music research. Sam's in those days was a very humble country pub, with wooden tables and benches, where the locals would order a 'boiler' at the bar, a mixture of brown ale and mild. As we walked in, we spied George, who sat in the corner with his flat cap, tweed jacket, and bow-tie, playing the melodeon. He greeted us warmly and thus started a series of trips to Sam's to hear and record George and to play along with him. George was a well-known character in the area, who in his younger days had mixed with show-people and Gypsy folk, learning step-dance tunes and Gypsy speech from them. Step-dancing was once common throughout England. This is a solo dance, usually done to a brisk hornpipe rhythm, with elaborate foot taps, and is related to tap dancing in general, as in the old Fred Astaire films. In southern and eastern England, it is usually danced to brisk hornpipe or polka tunes, of which George played a number. His impressive features and broad Hampshire accent were such that, without him showing off at all, the musical life of the pub naturally centred on him. George was an impressive and showy spoons player, and his melodeon-playing was forceful with a rare vigour and style, but usually at full volume and not subtle or technically precise. In fact, it was said that he never owned a melodeon of his own but always played a borrowed one. The pub kept an instrument under a wooden bench for him to play. Whenever I lent him my melodeon, I was worried that his huge hands would break a reed!

Like most country musicians, his repertoire was very eclectic. Most of the tunes he played were the sing-along numbers that he had grown up with, such as 'Daisy, Daisy', 'Yes, Sir, That's My Baby', and even tunes picked up from the folk revival such as 'The Leaving of Liverpool'. From time to time he would launch into step-dance hornpipe tunes and say with a grin, 'Who'll give a step-dance, then?', or else an old jig, waltz, or march. He acted as a magnet for singers and musicians, both revival and traditional, in the area. On one occasion, I was lucky enough to witness three traditional melodeon players all playing away in the bar.

As a singer, George always promised more than he delivered, and getting songs out of him was frustrating. He had a strong voice but couldn't be described as a good singer – he rarely sang a song all the way through and often stopped in the middle of a song, complaining that he 'couldn't get it tonight'. My attempts and the efforts of others to get him to sing were usually exasperating, as he was a person who, although extremely friendly, would let you into his world only a little at a time. There was an occasion when Carol and I spent a whole evening with him in a pub and collected just one song – at a verse every half-hour! He would sing a verse, play some more music, and then would say, 'Oh, there's another verse.' And so, over the course of one evening, we noted his fine version of 'Three Men Went a-Hunting':

> *Three men went a-hunting, and nothing could they find*
> *Until they came to a hedgehog and that they left behind*
> *The Englishman said, 'It's a hedgehog', the Scotsman he said, 'Nay'*
> *Paddy said, 'It's a pincushion with the pins turned t'other way'*
> *For 'twas half past five in the morning in the middle of the night*
> *The ducks began to quarrel, and the pigs began to fight*
> *The neighbours looked out of the window to see that all was right*
> *For 'twas half past five in the morning in the middle of the night.*

Plus several more verses.

George Privett playing at the Barleycorn Inn, Bishop's Waltham, Hampshire. Photo by courtesy of Chris Sullivan.

George played music until well into his latter days. In the mid-1970s he teamed up with the traditional Devon melodeon player Ruth Askew, who lived in Hampshire, and for several years George and Ruth were a regular feature at a round of sympathetic pubs in the area. Here was a man who was a true folk artist, holding his own on familiar territory, and with his roots in an age when village and pub music-making was strong. Despite his rough melodeon playing and unfinished songs, George was my first folk hero and role model. More than that, he was a link in a long chain of tavern musicians who have kept us entertained for centuries.

Incidentally, Sam's Hotel is now a slightly upmarket country pub with a new name, a nice restaurant, and tinkling muzak. Despite the horse brasses and old photos, it just does not have the same atmosphere. If you go in Sam's and really concentrate, you can just about imagine the old boys pumping away on their melodeons on a Saturday night. But the bar staff don't know what a 'boiler' is any more. Nevertheless, some local folk musicians have established a regular step-dancing session there and so the pub once again resounds to melodeon and fiddle and the rap-a-tap of the step-dancers. Furthermore, George's spoons, dented with use, are in a glass case over the bar.

George was a great influence on Hampshire singer, musician, and researcher Paul Marsh, whose contribution to the folk scene is vastly underrated. Paul died suddenly and unexpectedly on St George's Day 2018 at the untimely age of sixty-seven. He steeped himself in the music still to be found in Hampshire pubs in the 1970s and 80s, and made some important recordings, both audio and video. He was also a tireless researcher of old recordings and assisted in the making of many source-performer CDs. His loss to the folk scene is immense, as he was a true link to the old traditions.

It was Paul who discovered the legendary Stan Seaman. Stan was a remarkable musician from Buckler's Hard in the New Forest, who learned the melodeon at the tender age of four and continued playing all his long life. He passed away in 2012 at the age of ninety-three. His career spanned the time when the big bands drove out the local village culture, sometime in the 1930s. Up until that time, at the Saturday-night dances in Buckler's Hard, the musicians would play first for a dance, and then there would be a song. One dance, one song, and so on throughout the evening. That was the old style, probably based on local custom that had been unchanged for many years. The music and dances of the big bands were no doubt very professional and glamorous, but they stamped out the old village ways overnight in that quiet corner of the New Forest. Nowadays, of course, we have got so used to the idea that music and song is best left to the professionals and the media. Of course, it's different in the folk music world…

One abiding memory of Stan is when he and Alf Riglar, another Hampshire old boy who played the melodeon, came to Gloucestershire for the English Country Music Weekend in the late 1990s. Stan and Alf knew very few of the tunes that the revival session musicians were playing, and really it should have been the session musicians listening to them, rather than vice versa. However, in the evening, a group of us took ourselves along to a small country pub just outside Cheltenham. Sat at on old church pew by an open fire, Stan and Alf got out their melodeons and played for the next three hours. It was nearly all sing-along material, the sort of repertoire that revival musicians do not play in their sessions, and it immediately took me back to Sam's Hotel with George Privett. The locals, including some travellers, thoroughly enjoyed it, and at the end of the evening, to our surprise, the landlady said, 'That was lovely. What do we owe you boys for the music?' I suggested a modest but realistic sum, which would pay for Stan and Alf's petrol and beer plus a bit more, and everyone went home happy. Which scenario was 'real' folk: the session musicians playing polkas and hornpipes or the old boys in the bar playing 'Daisy, Daisy' and 'Knees Up, Mother Brown'? The answer, of course, is both; but I'll let the reader ponder that question further.

I still make trips to Hampshire, mainly to visit relations, and try to return to some of those old haunts that bring back so many memories. A couple of years ago, I visited the Harrow with some cousins. John Dodd popped in and I prevailed upon him to sing 'Fathom the Bowl', and I gleefully told my cousins that our maternal grandfather had sung that same song. Also, on recent visits to the Harrow, I have managed to record some interesting songs from Davie, one of the locals, with a Hampshire accent that makes mine sound posh. And so the collecting goes on.

I'll Give You the Waysailing Bowl, the Gloucestershire Waysailing Bowl

My move to Gloucestershire in the early 1970s was not too traumatic. The locals were friendly, and their speech even sounded a bit like Hampshire, but without the whiff of Cockney or Estuary English that was starting to infiltrate Portsmouth speech by then. Having been bitten by the collecting bug, I decided that Gloucestershire had to be a good place to try, but my first enquiries were not promising. One local, who was a big name on the local folk scene, informed me that it was a waste of time trying to collect, as there were no more traditional singers to be found in the county, and if anyone told him that there were old boys still singing folk songs in Gloucestershire pubs, then he would not believe them. I can look back on that conversation now, having made many hours of recordings in Gloucestershire, and gloat. I was still inexperienced in my recording techniques but did the best I could. If only I could re-record all those old singers now!

With the help of some members of the folk community, I did start to discover singers, starting with

Dick Parsons, a real old Gloucestershire character with accent to match, who used a pub not five miles from me as his local. Although my recordings of Dick are in a very noisy environment, it was he who first put me on to asking about the wassail. Dick thrilled me as he described how in his younger days, he had gone around the Hatherley and Reddings area, on the outskirts of Cheltenham, on Boxing Day, with his brother and some other friends, carrying a wassail bowl and singing their version of the wassail song. They usually sang unaccompanied, but on the one occasion when they did take a melodeon, Dick's brother walked into a lamp-post whilst playing it and instantly doubled the number of melodeons he was holding. I am trying to picture him with half a melodeon in each hand! It was also Dick who told me that it should be pronounced 'waysail', and I have found this to be consistent in all the Gloucestershire versions that I have collected to date (about seven). Dick sang me several old country songs, including 'The Life of a Man' and a wonderful version of 'Barley Mow'. I lost sight of Dick for several years until I tracked him down again in indifferent health in a retirement home just around the corner from my house, where he sang me his version of the 'Seven Joys of Mary'. Or rather, he sang one verse and the chorus and recited the rest. He died shortly afterwards. Just like Arthur Baker and George Privett in Hampshire, Dick was one of a long line of the old country singers.

Another notable singer that we met in those days was Ray Hartland, a dairy farmer living to the west of Cheltenham. I never saw Ray when he didn't have a wide grin on his face, and he went through life with a chuckle and a positive attitude. His cider barn was an education. Carol and I took Mike Yates to record him, and, of course, the place where he felt most at home was in the barn. There, in between singing songs such as 'Billy Johnson's Ball' and 'The Ball of Yarn', he treated us, and himself, to copious samples of his potent home-made cider from a huge wooden vat, served in mugs fashioned from a cow's horn. It was the sort of scene that took you back to different times. I am pleased to report that Ray's two sons have carried on his cider-making tradition and they still sell it from the family farm.

I soon learned that in Gloucestershire it paid off to ask all the singers I met whether they knew 'The Waysailing Bowl', and in many cases my enquiry met with success. It transpired that nearly every village in and around the Stroud valley had its own version of the song, along with a variation of the custom. Typical of this was Billy Buckingham, then living in Stonehouse, who was one of the last of the waysailers that toured the area of Kingscourt and Woodchester, just south of Stroud. When Billy was about twelve years old, around the time of the First World War, he, his brother, and a friend learned their version of 'The Waysailing Bowl' and went around the farms and pubs before Christmas, singing their song and showing off the bowl. They wore women's clothes and blackened their faces and improvised the bowl by decorating a chamber pot. It should be stated at this point that the Gloucestershire wassail custom did not involve drinking from the pot. On a good night they would make £3, a huge sum in those days, and were also given the local Gloucestershire cider or 'scrumpy' at the farms they visited. Fancy giving cider to a child!

Billy could still be prevailed upon to perform the song in the pubs of Stonehouse in the 1970s. His performance was something to be witnessed, as he declaimed, rather than sang the song, his arms flailing and eyes flashing. He would always start this performance with a short preamble:

'When I was a young man in Gloucestershire, I used to go waysailing, round the best houses and the farms. I'll give you the Waysailing Bowl, the Gloucestershire Waysailing Bowl.'

Then he would launch into the song:

Waysail, waysail, over the town
Our cup it is white and our ale it is brown
Our bowl it is made of the white maple tree
To me waysailing bowl, I'll bring unto thee.

Some of the verses had lovely old Gloucestershire pronunciations in them:

> *Now here's health to my master and to his right arm*
> *Pray God send our master a good crop of carn [corn]*
> *And a good crop of carn and another of 'ay*
> *To pass the cold wintery wy-unds [winds] away.*

As the song progressed, the locals in the pub, many of them Billy's contemporaries, gradually joined in, and by the last verse all were singing their heads off:

> *There was an old woman, she had but one cow*
> *And how to maintain it she did not know how*
> *She builded a barn to keep her cow warm*
> *And a drop of your cider will do us no harm.*[1]

---

[1] Billy's performance of the Waysailing Bowl can be heard on the Topic Voice of the People CD *You lazy lot of bone-shakers* (TSCD666).

Billy Buckingham, the last of the Woodchester Wassailers, 1997.
Photo – Gwilym and Carol Davies

Carol and I subsequently revisited Billy in his home in Stonehouse, where we made a video recording of him talking about the wassail custom and singing the song.

Many people do not have a clear idea as to what wassailing, or 'waysailing', really means, which is not surprising, as it can take on different meanings in different contexts. Is it a drink, a song, or a custom?

Etymology will tell you that the word comes from old English '*Waes hael*', which means 'Be healthy', as in hale and hearty, and the phrase can be traced back a thousand years in literature, even getting a mention in *Beowulf*. So, in its original form it is a greeting, a blessing or a toast, to which the reply is '*Drinc hael*'. It is older than most of our English customs, and it is English, as, apart from isolated examples in the

Gower and the Mari Lwyd custom in Wales, it has no equivalent in the other countries of the British Isles. The history of wassailing is complex but looking at the various forms, it seems that in time it came to mean a midwinter blessing on crops, animals, and even on the farmers. At some point it divided into what you might call the 'standing still wassail' and the 'moving about wassail'. In the former, as practised in Somerset, Devon, and up in Herefordshire, it came to mean a blessing on the cider apple trees in particular, and elaborate practices grew up of going to an orchard, firing guns into the trees, leaving bread dipped in cider for the birds, and so on. The 'moving around' version of wassailing is the one practised in Gloucestershire, as well as other parts of the West Country. There is no evidence that the Gloucestershire version ever involved guns or apples. It was a door-to-door custom, notably at pubs, farms, and big houses, with the participants carrying a decorated bowl and singing the song. The bowl was central to the custom. It was not there to put drink or money in but was decorated with Christmas greenery. In Tresham and Tetbury, in the south of Gloucestershire, they even stood a small Christmas tree in the middle of the bowl. In some places in the south of the county the waysailers also took around with them a primitive type of hobby-horse known as 'the Broad', which represented a cow. The function of the Broad was to prance about and to frighten the occupants of the house. I like to think that at one time they took a real cow around with them, but perhaps the logistics became too much. The words of the Gloucestershire version all pay homage to the cow/bull/ox.

So, in Gloucestershire, the people did not 'hold a wassail' but went 'waysailing'. However, there is a growing trend for organising and holding wassails these days. The attraction is plain, in that you can get a lot of people together, have a good time, drink cider, dance the Morris, and sing songs. All very commendable. The elephant in the room is that often the organisers are under the impression that they are reviving an old Gloucestershire tradition, when what they are doing is inventing it. Again, nothing wrong with that, except when these events are seen by the public and the media and the participants as the 'real thing', and the old wassail is forgotten. The recently started large scale Stroud Wassail event, involving singers and Morris dancers, breaks the mould and has dispensed with the apple orchard part. It is very much a magnet for Morris sides, but it has made many aware of the old custom.

But wassail is only one strand of the folk song that was part of the fabric of life of old Gloucestershire. In my researches I came across scores of memories of Saturday-night sing-songs in country pubs, where music-hall and contemporary songs held sway amongst old English drinking songs, ballads, wartime ditties, and so on. In the closing years of the twentieth century, I found and recorded scores of singers in Gloucestershire. Not one regarded himself or herself as a 'folk singer', and, compared with Harry Cox or Walter Pardon, they were not. But they all had a song to sing and a tale to tell. The term 'folk song' seldom met with a response, but the term 'old song' often did. The singers were mainly active as performers in the decades before and after the Second World War, when parts of the county were still remote, had only dirt roads leading to them, and were seldom visited by outsiders. So, I was conscious of the fact that I was recording a remembered tradition rather than an active one.

There were exceptions, such as the musical evenings still taking place in, say, the Bisley House pub in Stroud or the Fox at Hawkesbury Upton, but by and large the moment had passed. I took the decision also to record as much of the repertoire as possible, including music-hall and well-known ditties. This was a different approach from other earlier collectors, who had just gone for what they regarded as the 'real' folk songs of a singer's repertoire. Whereas Cecil Sharp did not stop to pick primroses (referring to 'The Banks of Sweet Primroses') as they were too numerous to bother about, I was delighted to find someone who knew the song. Bob Copper, collecting in Hampshire in the 1950s, rarely noted 'All Jolly Fellows that Follow the Plough', as he naturally assumed that all his singers knew it, that it was too well-known and standardised to collect, and so he used the song himself as a conversational warm-up to more 'interesting' items in the repertoire. Peter Kennedy was averse to music-hall songs and recorded very few from his source singers, even though he must have heard many. I merrily went on my way, grateful for anything that the singers could sing to me, so long as it seemed to me to be part of the oral tradition.

As a result, I have a large collection of recordings of 'Buttercup Joe', probably all deriving from the 1928 recording by Albert Richardson, a song that Cecil Sharp, Bob Copper, and Peter Kennedy must have heard many times, but not considered worthy of collection. It got to the point that when I announced to my family that I was going to record yet another singer, my daughter would say to me, 'Please don't come back with another recording of "Buttercup Joe", Daddy.' I consider that this all-encompassing approach to collecting gives a much fuller and more revealing view of the role of the singer in his or her community. Traditional singers often have a different perspective on their songs from the revivalist or collector. Here's an example: I was very excited to record a version of 'Oh Mariners All', also known as 'A Jug of This', from one old singer, Ray Driscoll, of whom more anon. I knew that the song had not been collected in oral tradition for about a century and it was assumed that it had dropped out of circulation. Ray was as unexcited about it as I was excited. He referred to it as 'a bit of a bloody dirge', and so far as he was concerned, he had more interesting songs in his repertoire; whereas to me it was like finding a nugget of gold.

The iconic folk-song collector Mike Yates, who had done some impressive work on behalf of Topic Records, visited Gloucestershire in the late 1970s at the invitation of Rod and Rhona Smith, local musicians who had been recording the Gypsy singer Harry Brazil, but on a very basic cassette recorder and in noisy pub conditions.[2] Rod and Rhona were doing valuable groundwork, but they really wanted Mike's expertise to get good-quality recordings of Harry. This was the point at which I met Mike and we hit it off immediately, being on the same wavelength so far as folk song was concerned and sharing a similar sense of humour. For the next two years, Mike was a regular visitor from London to our house, travelling down on a Friday night, and then on the Saturday and Sunday I would take him to meet and record the various singers that I had discovered in the area. I learned a lot from Mike about how to get better-quality recordings, such as setting up the acoustics in order to get a 'clean' recording. Mike preferred to record in people's houses rather than pubs, to avoid background noise, and was very touchy about ticking clocks and other extraneous noises coming in on the recording. He always used a microphone stand and a high-quality microphone and tape recorder, so his recordings suffered none of the quality problems that mine did. I learned that the

[2] Rod and Rhona were kind enough to give me a copy of their tape, and it is well that they did, as their copy was destroyed when their flat was flooded. Their recordings will be passed on to the British Library Sound Archive.

collector should control the recording session, rather than the singer, and that it is all right to interrupt or to get the singer to start again if need be. Mike and I travelled throughout the county and beyond, recording Gypsy singers, traditional carols and wassails, ballads, and so on. As well as recording the singers that I had originally come across, we made further enquiries and found more singers. Our efforts were usually successful, but we were turned away by one slightly irate wife as the last time her husband had gone singing down the local pub, he had come back rather the worse for wear. No names, no pack drill.

We decided to visit the Hill/Bishop family at Bromsberrow Heath, where other collectors, notably Peter Kennedy and Russell Wortley, had already noted a few songs, particularly Christmas carols. The Hills were very receptive but had very few of the old carols. Their main singer was Ivor Hill, who sang us a delightful version of 'The Holly and the Ivy' and a very attractive carol called 'Carol, Carol Gaily', which I suspect is not a product of the folk mind at all, but very tuneful, nonetheless. Mike and I were dismayed to hear that shortly after our recording session Ivor Hill died in a traffic accident whilst riding his bicycle.

Mike was ever optimistic that we would find real gems of undiscovered folk song. He was always hoping that we would come across a version of 'Bold Sir Rylas' or 'The House Carpenter'. No such luck, but Mike did record versions of both those songs on his trips to the Appalachian Mountains.

Just to round off this chapter on my folk-song collecting in Gloucestershire, I should add that the folk music revival is very strong in the county, with Morris dancing, mummers, pub sessions, folk choirs, folk clubs, ceilidhs and several festivals. It is heartening that there are still many out there who have embraced folk culture and are developing it in their own way.

Dear Ol' Deb'n

Having close friends, Colin and Sonja Andrews, who lived in the centre of Devon and were keen on folk music, gave me opportunities to travel down and meet performers.

Carol and I were fortunate to attend the first Dartmoor Folk Festival in the little village of South Zeal (two pubs, one shop) in the 1970s, where we were thrilled to find that local musician Bob Cann had revived the step-dance competition. The festival and the competition are now well established, but then it was a revelation to us. Various locals took their turns to dance a series of steps on the back of a farm waggon, accompanied by concertina player Jimmie Cooper, playing local hornpipe tunes. The step-dancing then was not a competition as such but a demonstration, and afterwards we took the opportunity to talk to Jimmie about his tunes and recorded from him the 'Schottische Hornpipe' and 'Jack the Lad', a tune that Bob called 'Cokey's Hornpipe'. We followed up this chat with a visit to Jimmie's house shortly afterwards and recorded him playing the accordeon and singing snatches of songs.

Jimmie Cooper of South Zeal, Devon,
playing for step dancing in 1970.
Photo – Gwilym Davies

When I met Bob Cann again, I was smitten with his dynamic melodeon playing and his rich rolling Devon accent, which gave me a further insight into the folklore of the area. On one memorable occasion, Bob invited myself, my wife and a couple of friends to a lunchtime session with his old Cornish pal Charlie Bate, and the two of them put on a beautiful lunchtime concert of local songs and tunes in a little pub, with an audience of about ten people. I felt privileged.

Talking of step-dancing, on one visit to the Dartmoor Folk Festival I made the acquaintance of the Orchard family, namely Tommy and Jeannie Orchard and their sons, plus Jeannie's parents. Tommy is an expert step dancer and, at festival time, holds centre place in the music-making in the King's Arms, playing his melodeon and step-dancing on the piece of board which he brings with him for the purpose. Jeannie is a lovely singer and sings in the old Gypsy style, with some songs that she learnt from her mother, the magnificent Amy Birch. I once had the privilege of recording Amy in her trailer and she sang me some of her family songs such as her version of 'The Lakes of Cool Finn' and 'The Molecatcher'. I felt I was in the presence of something special, hearing eighty-year-old Amy recount songs that stretched back to her younger days.

On one trip to Devon, I was told that I really had to meet Charlie Hill of Dartmoor, and I was introduced to him one evening in a country pub. Charlie was an absolute delight and was not only keen to sing me his songs, he was insistent on it. Over the next few years, I made a point of calling in on Charlie whenever I visited Devon and recorded some of his songs, of which he seemed to have an endless repertoire. I gathered, from talking to him, that he had grown up hearing folk songs from his family and other locals, but it was not until he started going to the folk club at Exeter and plucking up the courage to sing that he, and the folk world, realised how many local songs he knew. In fact, unlike many of the source singers I met, his repertoire was largely what we would call folk songs.

Charlie was a great talker, although sometimes you had to keep up with him, as his thoughts jumped from subject to subject, but I made a point of asking him where he had learned his songs. Many of them were from the local Gypsy families that used to call in on his father's farm, and the Hill family obviously had a healthy respect for them and their songs. Like Bob Cann, Charlie's speech was the old Devon accent, which is rarely heard these days.

Charlie was very keen to supplement his repertoire by seeking out words to half-remembered songs. I gather that he obtained words for some of his songs from the folk-song collector Paul Wilson, and presumably then sang them to the tune he knew. For example, he gave me two different tunes he had learned for 'The Quarrelsome Wife', an amusing ditty of a husband trying to swap chores with his wife for the day and failing utterly. Charlie only knew four verses, which he sang to me, and asked if I had a complete set of words. I duly supplied him with a set from the Fred Hamer collection, and the next time I went down to Devon he was singing the complete song.

Charlie Hill – traditional Dartmoor singer.
Photo – Gwilym Davies

I know I am not the only person to record Charlie, and that Paul Wilson and Sam Richards and Tish Stubbs also made recordings of him, but to date those recordings have not been issued. Bob and Jackie Patten also made recordings of Charlie, with interesting interviews, which are available to hear on the British Library Sound Archive website. From what I learned from talking to Charlie and looking more deeply into the folk songs and tunes of Devon, I have formed the impression that the county was a stronghold for traditional songs way into the twentieth century, whereas they had been fading away in many other areas of the country. As a postscript to this chapter, I recently attended a very good pub-singing session in Devon and announced that I would sing some of Charlie's songs, but was disappointed that not one of the assembled folkies had heard of him. Such is fame.

Kids, Don't You Just Love 'Em

I am happy to record songs from anyone, so long as I feel that they are not songs that they have learned directly from books or records. What I am after is the real folklore within a person, without the influence of the media. In this respect, children's songs are a fascinating source of research. However, even here media influence is all-pervasive. Collections of children's songs and games from a hundred years ago, and even field recordings made fifty years ago, indicate a long line of tradition, and kids today still sing in the playground, but most of the old singing games and rhymes have gone, along with skipping ropes. Many of the rhymes have been replaced by snatches of songs from television adverts. Also, performing these rhymes is almost always confined to girls in the seven to ten age range. After that age, it is not 'cool' to sing playground rhymes.

All this is a drastic simplification of the situation, but I decided to put it to the test by asking my seven-year-old daughter to tell me all the playground rhymes that she came across. We started a book, 'Mary-Ann's Song Book', and most weeks she would find a new rhyme to go into it. It was necessary to work quickly as a rhyme remembered one day would be forgotten the next, so we wrote down the rhymes while they were still warm, so to speak. The songs that went into 'Mary-Ann's Song Book' were certainly not what Miss Pringle had taught us, but they have a charm of their own:

I went to a Chinese chip shop to buy a loaf of bread
They wrapped it up in a five-pound note and this is what they said
My name is ipsi-ipsi, girls are sexy
Sitting in the back row, drinking Pepsi
How's your father? – All right
Died in the fish shop – Last night
What did he die of? – Bad fish
Where did he get it? – Your dish!

Down by the bramble bushes, down by the sea
True love for you, my darling, true love for me
When we get married, we'll raise a family
A boy for you, a girl for me.
How many fishes in the sea?
Twelve and twelve make twenty-four
Kick your teacher out the door
If he does not understand that
Hit him on the head with a baseball bat.
Teacher, teacher, I declare
I can see your underwear

Is it black or is it white?
Oh my gosh, it's dynamite.
Ten, nine, eight, seven, six, five, four, three, two,
one
Blast Off!

Some of the rhymes indicated a certain antiquity:

My boyfriend gave me an apple
My boyfriend gave me a pear
My boyfriend gave me a kiss on the lips
And threw me down the stair, stair, stair.
I gave him back his apple
I gave him back his pear
I gave him back his kiss on the lips
And threw him down the stair, stair, stair.

It may come as a shock to some parents that their offspring are obsessed with bums and knickers:

Mrs Brown went to town
With her knickers falling down.

It is also interesting to note what word the children use to declare a pause in a game. Around Cheltenham, it's 'Crusy' or even 'Crusade'. Where I grew up in Portsmouth a cry of 'Scribs', along with crossed fingers, would be enough to give you a pause for a breather in the game. Every area has its own word.

I obtained permission on one occasion to go to my daughter's primary school to record songs in the playground. My worries that I would not find any were quickly allayed as the children, mainly girls, literally queued up to tell me their rhymes, mainly to accompany handclapping, skipping or 'elastic', the latter involving jumping over a long string of elastic while reciting the rhymes. The only actually singing games that came to light were 'Ring a Ring a Roses', 'Here We go around the Mulberry Bush' and 'The Farmer's in his Den', but there were a number of counting-out rhymes, as well as the epic 'When Susie was a Baby', recounting Susie's life from birth to afterlife as a ghost. In a fifteen-minute recording session, I had enough material for a small booklet, which was sold to raise funds for the PTA.

Television has been a particular culprit in changing children's folklore. In small ways it has added to it, by supplying a stream of jingles that are ripe for parody, but in other ways it has killed it. I was told that in Portugal the village children at one time used to spend two or three hours every evening in the village square playing singing games. That tradition was lost overnight when television arrived in the villages. Television, if you like, robbed them of their heritage. Change is inevitable, but with television you are leading out someone else's life, hopes, fears, and ambitions, not your own. Ewan MacColl referred to television as 'encouraging us to live our lives in the flickering half-light of someone else's dreams', and for all the good things it brings in giving us a window on the world, we tend to forget our own life and culture. Most modern pubs have a television, usually on with the volume turned down, as though the customers might suffer withdrawal symptoms if the box is not flickering away in the corner of the room. That may well be true – how would many families cope if television were taken away from them? Many would have nothing to say, as they have lost their culture to the goggle-box.

Some Outstanding Characters:

1. Ray Driscoll

Traditional folk-singers come in many shapes and forms. They are as varied as humanity itself. Some will be shy, some extrovert, some illiterate, some highly educated, some who 'just sing', and some who are acutely aware of the inheritance that they carry around in their heads. Some understand musical syntax, and some do not (mainly not). Some are intelligent and some less so. Some have one song, and some have large repertoires. Some are ingenuous, and some are pretentious. All are interesting and have a tale to tell.

Every now and then the folk world, or rather the twilight world of folk-song collectors, comes across an important singer who has been overlooked or undiscovered, although the chances of more such discoveries in England are now practically nil. Ray Driscoll was one such singer. Ray was 'discovered' when someone whose identity I don't know tipped off Mike Yates in the early 1990s that Ray had been heard singing some interesting songs at a party in London. Mike visited Ray and recorded some songs from him, including the mysterious 'Wild, Wild Berry':

Young man came from hunting, faint and weary
'What ails my lord, my dearie?'
'Oh, mother dear, let my bed be made
Of the leaves and berries of the woody nightshade.'
Lie low, sweet Randal.
So, come all you young men that do eat full well
And they that sup right merry.
'Tis far better, I entreat, to have toads for your meat
Than to eat of the wild, wild berry.

Now this young man, he died eft soon
By the light of the hunter's moon.
'Twas not by bolt nor yet by blade
But the deadly gripe of the woody nightshade.
Lie low, sweet Randal.
So, come all you young men that do eat full well
And they that sup right merry.
'Tis far better, I entreat, to have toads for your meat
Than to eat of the wild, wild berry.

This lord's false love, they hanged her high
For her deeds were the cause of her love to die
And in her hair, they entwined a blade
Of the leaves and berries of the woody nightshade.
Lie low, sweet Randal.
So, come all you young men that do eat full well
And they that sup right merry.
'Tis far better, I entreat, to have toads for your meat

Than to eat of the wild, wild berry.

It is the only version of this song that has ever come to light and its origins are unknown. My theory is that a literary hand reworked the original 'Lord Randal' story, but there seems to be no way of proving it.

Mike Yates then put me on to Ray, and in 1993 I went to visit him at his home in Dulwich. I was immediately impressed by the friendly welcome Ray and his wife Sheila, a lovable cockney, extended to me. That afternoon I recorded a dozen or so songs from Ray, including the rare ballad 'The Death of Queen Jane', about the death of Henry VIII's third wife, Jane Seymour. In history, Jane died a fortnight after the birth of their son, Edward, but why spoil a good story with the facts? The folklore is much more interesting. In the song, Jane dies in childbirth after a caesarean section and Henry goes into mourning.

From that first meeting, Ray and I became firm friends and I became his companion and chaperone for various folk festivals in England. His crowning triumph came early in his 'professional' singing career when he was booked for the prestigious National Folk Festival in Loughborough and shared the stage with the famous McPeake family from Northern Ireland. For years afterwards, he would tell people how he was on the same bill as the McPeakes.

Ray had led a varied and interesting life. He was born into a military family in County Mayo in 1922. His Irish father, who was in the army, played the fiddle and taught Ray his first folk songs, such as 'My Bonny Boy', an Irish version of 'Long a-Growing'. Ray then moved to Shropshire. His time there left him with a deep love of the wild and mysterious countryside and its people. Throughout his life he absorbed songs from all sources. Whilst still a lad in Shropshire he bumped into the itinerant farm labourer Harry Civil, although he suspected that the epithet 'Civil' was bestowed upon Harry as a joke, as civility was not a characteristic usually associated with him. While the other lads of the area shunned Harry and his wild ways, young Ray was fascinated by his tales and songs. It was from Harry that Ray learned the 'Wild, Wild Berry' and 'The Death of Queen Jane', in return for the odd bottle of beer. Ray's first wife was from Shropshire, and through her family he was introduced to another repertoire of songs, including a more conventional 'Lord Randal', 'The Banks of Sweet Primroses', and snatches of wassailing and soul-caking songs.

Time in the Royal Navy during the Second World War, flitting between Scapa Flow and Portsmouth, added more songs to his repertoire, and when he settled in London to work in the printing trade, he picked up even more songs, including music-hall snatches and street songs. Ray also spent time in Wigan amongst the Irish community, adding further to his repertoire, including a rare satirical song about the defeat of Napoleon, entitled 'Pompalerie Jig'. Ray learned this song from an Irish singer who apparently sang it so often that they nicknamed him 'Pompey'. Ray's is the only version of the song that has come to light, but it seems to be of some antiquity. In the song, the British army defeats Napoleon, not by guns or regiments, but solely by their 'Pompalerie Jig', which seems to stand for something like 'swagger' or 'attitude'. There is a sardonic twist in the last verse:

> *And how did they serve the veterans that did this daring deed?*
> *They published them a vagrancy act to furnish all their needs*
> *Passed by act of Parliament, by the Tories and the Whigs*
> *And they left us all with nothing but a Pompalerie Jig.*

Ouch! The phrase 'Pompalerie Jig' also appears in a children's counting-out rhyme, so presumably at one time it had some currency in popular speech:

> *Zeenty teenty feggery fell, pompalerie jig.*
> *Every man who has no hair generally wears a wig.*

Ray was also a good amateur wrestler in his time. He fought in many amateur matches and recounted that he occasionally fought Jackie Pallo, who went on to become a famous television wrestler. Ray had a low opinion of Jackie's wrestling ability and said that getting drawn against him in a competition was as good as getting a bye. Ray maintained his strength until late in life, and at a health check-up when he was in his sixties the unsuspecting medic asked Ray to squeeze his hand as hard as he could. Ray first asked him, 'Are you sure?', and on being given the go-ahead, nearly cracked the poor doctor's bones.

Ray always took a great interest in folk songs and folk culture, to the extent that he and Sheila were regular visitors to the May Day celebrations at Padstow in Cornwall, where they met up with other singers, including enthusiastic folk-singing friends from Edenbridge, in Kent, who were intrigued by his songs. Ray was a very likeable man, who charmed wherever he went. He had a knack of getting on with people. In Gloucestershire he met up with the Gypsy Wiggy Smith, described in another chapter in this book, and they bonded extremely well from the start, mainly because of their shared interest in boxing and wrestling.

As a singer, Ray sang with a natural lilt and charm, usually with a hint of his Irish background, even when singing songs he had learned in Shropshire. He had a keen and enquiring mind, and although he would not have described himself as an academic, he was always interested to hear different versions of songs and to look a little deeper into them. He was a veritable sponge for songs, and even in his late seventies he was learning new ones. From me he learned 'The Bold Poacher' and 'Green Bushes', which immediately took on a fresh tone and style when he performed them. As well as learning new songs, he continually remembered old ones. After hearing the group Brass Monkey perform a supposedly rare Irish version of 'Soldier, Soldier, Won't You Marry Me' at the Cheltenham Folk Festival, he commented, 'Well, that's not a rare song. I know that.' The result was that the same evening I recorded Ray singing his version of the song. Such is folklore, and such is human memory. He probably would not have thought of singing me that song had he not heard it at the concert.

*Ray Driscoll in
Padstow, 1999.
Photo – Gwilym Davies*

Ray worked for many years in the printing trade in London, and in his later years, after his wife had retired, he moved from London to Shropshire, where he lived out his days. I was honoured to be asked to sing at his funeral and chose one of his songs, 'The Banks of Sweet Primroses', a song of love, hope, and springtime.

2. Gordon Hall

Many people knew Gordon Hall much better than I did, but my few meetings with him made a huge impression on me. When he turned up at the London Inn in Padstow on May Day 1995, he soon became a focus of attention, talking about songs, singing snatches of them, and generally entertaining all around. And that was Gordon – he could not help being the centre of attention, but naturally and without effort.

The following year I visited him in the company of Ray Driscoll and we spent a day talking to Gordon, or should I say listening to him, as he was a very articulate speaker with a fund of knowledge and love of folk songs. You didn't have to prompt him to talk about songs and singing. Over the course of a few hours he told us how he had learned many songs from his mother, Mabs Hall. Mabs and Gordon had already been visited by several folk-song collectors, including Mike Yates and John Howson, and Gordon was also in the habit of making tapes of his songs to send to interested parties, such as Roy Palmer, who was compiling a book of army songs.

Gordon regaled us at great length with his views on singers, meeting the Copper family, old Sussex songs, and so on. He sang many snatches of songs, but we had to pin him down from time to time to sing something all the way through. It was interesting to hear him talk about how his family would sing the songs – for example, he told us that the song 'Broomfield Hill' would be sung as a sort of duet, with men and women singing alternate verses. Throughout the meeting, and indeed throughout the songs, he chain-smoked, so that his performances were punctuated with puffs on his cigarette:

> *Lord Beckett was a noble lord-ah* [puff]
> *A noble lord of high degree-ah* [puff].

The slow speed at which he sang, plus his habit of repeating the last two lines of every verse, and the fact that he supplemented his songs from his large collection of broadsides, meant that his versions of songs were longer than everyone else's. When he announced to me that he wanted to sing 'Lord Beckett', a glance at my recorder showed that I had twenty-two minutes of tape left. Plenty, I thought; but as verse followed verse, I started to get worried. Eventually, the song ended at seventeen minutes, and I noted afterwards that he ended on the same pitch as the start of the song. It was an epic performance and left Ray and me speechless.

He often mentioned his brother Albert (yes, Albert Hall) who was living in Bayeux, in France, and whom he rated highly as a singer. On a subsequent visit to France, my wife and I called in on Albert and his French wife, and while Carol went off to visit the Bayeux Tapestry, I asked Albert about his family songs. There were a few surprises – Albert gave me a different impression of the family singing, which seemed to have been a lot less frequent than Gordon had led me to believe. Albert was of the view that much of what Gordon sang was when he was living alone with his mother Mabs, rather than being sung by the whole family. The only complete song I extracted from Albert was a racy version of 'The Bastard King of England', but he knew nothing of the 'family songs' such as 'The Leaves of Life' which Gordon had mentioned. Thus, I had two quite different versions of the Hall family singing context from two brothers. Such is folk.

Gordon was a total sponge for songs, with a phenomenal memory and a great rich voice. He seemed to recall song after song and had versions of most of the songs I mentioned to him. The world is a duller place without him.

3. Bob Arnold

For many people, an iconic sound was, and still is, the tune 'Barwick Green', composed by Arthur Wood, as it is the music that introduces and ends episodes of *The Archers*. Equally iconic was the voice heard on Sunday mornings on the radio introducing the omnibus edition of the programme with a cheery 'Morning all'. He was known to many as Tom Forrest, but that was his acting name. His real name was Bob Arnold. He was born and brought up in his beloved Oxfordshire and retained that rural burr in his rich speaking voice.

By his mid-twenties Bob was a regular entertainer at village concerts and parties, and was talent-spotted by the BBC, for which he sang Cotswold folk songs, some of them learned in his father's pub at Asthall, in Oxfordshire. In 1951 he joined the cast of *The Archers* and remained with them almost until his death in 1998. I visited him several times in his home in Burford in the 1990s and recorded several songs from him. Collectors Francis Collinson and Peter Kennedy had previously recorded a few songs from him, and he had made an LP of his songs with the Yetties, but I felt that no one had systematically attempted to note his repertoire. Subsequent to my visit, he was recorded by

Bob and Jackie Patten, seasoned folk-song collectors from Devon.

Bob Arnold was a very engaging person and was delighted that someone was taking an interest in his old songs. Apart from learning a lot of his songs in his father's pub, he also took an interest in the folk songs collected in the area by Alfred Williams. Williams was not a musician – he noted the words of over eight hundred songs, but frustratingly no tunes. Many of them were published in the 1920s in the *Wilts and Gloucester Standard*. Bob proudly showed me a scrapbook of cuttings of these publications and told me he was intrigued enough to set out and find the tunes. Thus, he recovered the missing tunes for several of the songs published by Williams, including 'Needle Cases'. He was also encouraged by the collector Harry Albino, who probably passed songs on to him, and he had a folder of Harry's collecting. He kindly allowed me to borrow the collection, which I photocopied and passed on a copy to the Vaughan Williams Memorial Library. I am happy to note that the collection is now online as part of the Vaughan Williams Memorial Library Digital Archive. He was still in fine voice in his eighties and was pleased to sing for me. Most of his songs were the real old country songs such as 'All Jolly Fellows that Follow the Plough' or 'Jim the Carter's Lad', but I was very surprised when he came out with a very rude monologue about a 'F**ting Contest', which presumably he had learned in the armed forces. If you want to hear it, you will have to go online.

On occasions when my local Morris dance team

went to Burford, he would join us in the pub and sing – in fact, it was difficult to stop him once he started, but we loved his company and were pleased to have had that connection with him.

4. Archer Goode

In the early 70s, when Carol and I moved into our first real house in Cheltenham, a modest two-bedroom semi, we had a small patch of lawn and an ageing lawnmower donated by generous parents. It soon became apparent that the mower would not cut the mustard, let alone the grass. A tip-off from a neighbour told us to call on a gentleman living in the next street who was an expert at restoring mowers. We accordingly knocked on his door and yes, he was willing to sharpen the machine, and a few days later it was returned in pristine condition.

Imagine our surprise on attending the Cheltenham Folk Club and hearing our neighbour sing a couple of old songs. On further enquiry, we were told that his name was Archer Goode and that he was a regular at the club, singing an older repertoire than the other club singers. My ears immediately pricked up, as I sensed someone who might know some older folk songs, and so we struck up an acquaintance which continued over several years.

Archer's family was from Herefordshire, where he was born in 1906 and they later moved to Abergavenny. He spent his early years in Abergavenny and married there. His speech always betrayed a slight Welsh lilt along with a rich country accent. He eventually moved to Cheltenham, where he lived until his death in 1984.

There were two elements that dominated Archer's life, namely his agricultural background and his love of singing. As a singer, he had picked up songs all his life, and he remembered with affection the songs he had learnt from Sam Bennett, the Ilmington Morris dancer, singer and musician, who often visited Abergavenny on holiday and would delight in entertaining the locals with songs, fiddle tunes and a broom dance.

As Archer lived so near, Carol and I spent several evenings calling on him and recording songs. The first song he sang to us was 'No, John, no', which he had learnt from Sam Bennett. He insisted that Sam always sang it as a duet, choosing a lady from the audience to sing with him. He therefore wrote out the words and got Carol to sing the female verses of the song. This was followed by other songs from Sam, including 'Jockie to the Fair' and 'Jan's Courtship'. Archer was also very proud of the songs that he had written, with echoes of his farming background, working with horses and crops, as well as songs of nostalgia of times gone by. Like several of the people I have recorded, Archer would tape his singing on a reel-to-reel recorder and would lend me the tapes to dub.

In about 1980, we took the collector Mike Yates to meet Archer and he recorded further songs, including a good version of 'The Life of a Man' and a verse of the ubiquitous 'Unquiet Grave'.

Despite Archer's years, he always sang with a clear, confident, unhurried style which echoed an earlier way of singing, and was always a pleasure to listen to.

Mandi Went to Puv the Grai (Gypsies)

Everyone has a view of Gypsies, often negative. Few understand or appreciate their way of life. It is to most people a closed world, one that on the one hand conjures up a romantic picture of freedom and the open air, and on the other hand an untrustworthy set of people to be avoided at all costs. By the same token, Gypsies, or travellers as they prefer to be known, have a suspicion of any non-Gypsy, or *gorgio*, to use the Romany word, peering too closely into traveller life. There are many misconceptions about the Gypsy way of life by those who do not or choose not to understand it. Gypsies are known colloquially as 'the travelling people', but in fact most English Gypsies these days live in the area in which they were born and will only travel around occasionally, and then only to visit relatives. We *gorgios* are the travelling people. If you ask a roomful of non-Gypsies how many of them are living in the county in which they were born, I guarantee that only about ten to fifteen per cent would say yes; with Gypsies it would be about ninety per cent.

In pre-industrial times, Gypsies had a strong symbiotic relationship with the farmers, turning up when labour was needed for crop-picking, or buying and selling horses. Now the crops are picked by machine or by foreign labour and farm horses are a thing of the past. So, Gypsies have had to fall back on trades where they use their practical skills, such as scrap-metal dealing, tarmacing drives, or tree surgery. This has meant that Gypsies have been pushed further back to the fringes of society and are held accountable for all sorts of misdemeanours. 'Respectable' folk seem to forget that Gypsies do not hold a monopoly on bad behaviour. According to my observations, bad behaviour seems evenly distributed throughout society. I am a great believer in the idea that people treat you as you treat them. I have always treated Gypsies (and everyone else, I hope) with great respect, and have always been met with friendliness from them. However, I can see that if as a people you have been mistreated and despised over centuries, you are likely to build up an attitude and a hard exterior.

I gradually became aware, mainly through the recordings that Mike Yates had made for Topic Records, of the importance that English Gypsies have, or should it be had, for our traditions. I knew no local Gypsies, but was aware of a nearby pub, between Cheltenham and Gloucester, that was frequented by Gypsies, being located right outside an established Gypsy campsite. So, with my friend Charlie, himself an undiscovered traditional singer, we determined to do some research. This consisted of going along to the pub one evening, armed with melodeon and whistle, and regaling the locals in the bar with a couple of hours of tunes, interspersed with 'Who's going to give us a song, then?' Apart from boozy versions of 'Can you Rokka Romany?' and 'Mandi Went to Puv the Grai',[3] both songs in the Romany-inflected language that travellers use, and the Dubliners' version of 'Seven Nights Drunk', our efforts came to naught – until the very end of the evening, when one of the Gypsies came over to us and said in a hoarse voice that if we wanted to know about songs, he would lend us a book with all his family songs. Charlie went over to the campsite and came back with a home-produced, typewritten book entitled 'Songs and Ballads of the Brazil Family of Gloucester', with the words of fifty folk songs, each one a gem. That person with the hoarse voice was Danny Brazil.

Charlie and I carefully photocopied the book and returned it to Danny. I say carefully, as we did not want to incur the wrath of a traveller family by damaging or losing the book. Danny could not have been more co-operative, and when I returned the book to him a week later, he said, 'I suppose you want to know the tunes.' This was like asking the Pope if he was Catholic. The first song that Danny sang to me was 'The Banks of Sweet Dundee', and he rather confused me at first by announcing that Dundee was in Ireland. Danny's hoarse voice was apparently the result of a family fight some years beforehand, but if he had had his full voice,

---

[3] Literally, 'Can you speak Romany?' and 'I put the horse [*grai*] in the field [*puv*]', meaning that the Gypsy would let his horse graze, illegally, of course, overnight in a farmer's field.

I am sure that he would have been one of the folk-song finds of the century, as he knew song after song, which he was keen to sing to me. It wasn't just that he was willing to sing, he was insistent on singing and fiercely proud of his repertoire. To him, it was vitally important to pass on these songs and to ensure that they were preserved. Despite his voice, he sang with clear tune and diction, and with a rare dignity.

One of the first songs he sang to me was the gripping supernatural ballad usually known as 'The Cruel Ship's Carpenter', and he startled me by announcing that he was going to sing 'The Seamen Song'. I wrongly assumed I was about to hear some previously uncollected item of English erotica! When the song started, 'Our captain wanted seamen, to sail on the sea', all was explained. Danny's gruff voice added to the drama of the song, which is a tale of boy meets girl, boy gets girl pregnant, boy kills girl, and runs away to sea. I remember the hairs on the back of my neck bristling when he got to the verse:

Earlie next morning at the dawn of the day
Our captain cried, 'Order, all hands come this
way
There's a murderer on board our ship and it's
latelye been done
Our ship is in mourning and she cannot sail on.'

This must be a piece of old maritime folklore. In

the last verse, the ghost of the wronged girl has her revenge on her seducer and murderer:

> *But as he was turning from his captain's command*
> *He saw pretty Polly all dressed up in white.*
> *She ripped him, she stripped him, she tore him all three*
> *Was because that he had murdered both baby and she.*

In later years, as Danny's voice started to go and he had problems remembering the words, one could sense the frustration welling up within him. But his contribution to folk song is enormous.

Back to the mysterious typewritten book. It was clear that someone had spent a lot of time recording these songs, but the mystery was who and when? It was some years before we, the folk community in Gloucestershire, discovered that the collector was one Peter Shepheard, a Gloucestershire man who was by then living in Scotland. Peter had spent some time in about 1966 seeking out Gypsy singers and recording them, unbeknown to the folk community in the area. I later got to meet him and hear some of the marvellous recordings that he made, but by then his interests had moved on to Scottish traditional music. However, all's well that ends well, and through the efforts of the tireless Rod Stradling and his one-man company Musical Traditions, these recordings are at long last coming to light and available to all on CD.

Danny's singing and approach to folk song taught me many things. I had assumed that as the words of the songs were in Peter's book, then Danny would sing one verse to me and say, 'There you are, that's the tune to that one'; but no, he insisted on singing each song all the way through, even the epic twenty-five-verse 'Lord Bateman'. It was just as well that he did so, as often the tune for the opening verse would be subtly different from the following verses. For Danny, a song was an entirety, not just a happy coming together of a tune and some verses. It was a whole experience. Carol and I took Mike Yates to meet Danny, and Mike was very happy to pick items from Danny's repertoire that he particularly wanted to record, namely the big Child ballads 'Edward' and 'The Cruel Mother', as well as 'Lord Bateman'.

In many ways, I was going over previously tilled ground by recording Danny, but as is the usual experience with collectors revisiting sources, Danny recalled songs that he had not remembered when Peter recorded him. One of the most remarkable was 'The Schoolmaster's Son', a short song that has only been noted twice in tradition, both times from Gypsies in Gloucestershire. Cecil Sharp collected a version in 1921 from the Gypsy Kathleen Williams at Wigpool Common in the Forest of Dean, and now, over fifty years later, I was committing it to tape for the first time from a living traditional singer:

When I was a young girl, a young girl at home
My parents they sent me to school
Till I became overcourted all by a false young man
That was all by my schoolmaster's son.

Then my parents they turned me out of doors, out
of doors
Was because that my character was gone.
It never would have been, if it wasn't for him
That was all by my schoolmaster's son.

As I was a-walking up Great London Street
You have heard of the same and before
Who should I chance to spy but my own true love
Where my thoughts would never would [sic] have
been.

For he tiled me an apple along of the floor
He was thinking to 'tice me once more.
I tiled it back again, straight back to him again
'Your apple, it's rotten to the core.'

'Come hold up your head, pretty maid, pretty maid
Come hold up your head, don't cry, dear
We'll have wedding bells to ring, we'll have
college girls to sing
We'll have tied hands all on our wedding day.'

My meetings with Danny led me on to meet his brother Harry and sister Lementina (Lemmie), who lived on a permanent site at Sandhurst, just north of Gloucester. Harry was one of the sweetest singers I had met, with an easy relaxed tenor voice, and I regret that I did not record more of his songs. Fortunately, Mike Yates managed to get most of his best songs down in one visit to Gloucester. Lemmie was quite a character, and the first time I met her on the door of her trailer she happily chatted away, telling me bits of her life story. She was charming and willingly played her melodeon for me. Her tunes consisted of old hornpipes, marches, waltzes, song tunes, and so on, many of them probably learnt in her younger days in Ireland, where she used to play for dancing and then collect a few coins as reward. Some of the tunes were very familiar, such as 'Soldier's Joy', 'Cock of the North', 'The Manchester Hornpipe', and so on, but she had some unusual items. One of the hornpipes she played is now common currency in English folk sessions as 'Lemmie's Number Two', but few realise that it was through me that it came to be known.

I lost contact with Danny for a while but met him again in the 1990s when recording songs from another Gypsy, Wiggy Smith. At this time, Wiggy and Danny lived just a few trailers apart on the same campsite at Elmstone Hardwicke, between Cheltenham and Tewkesbury. Wiggy had the utmost respect for Danny, almost twenty years his senior, and referred to him as 'Uncle Danny'. At that time Danny was in his late eighties and his health was failing, but his brain was still sharp, and he was most insistent that I continue to record him. He was fiercely proud of the heritage that he was passing on to me, and I do my best to keep it going and to respect it. When I told him that I had sung one of his songs somewhere, he retorted, 'Remember, you learnt that song from *me*.'

The two biggest Gypsy families in Gloucestershire are the Brazils and the Smiths, both of whom had large repertoires of old songs. Through the 1990s, my good friend Paul Burgess and I spent many hours in the company of Wiggy Smith, often cycling from work in our lunch hours to meet him at his favourite pub in the St Paul's area of Cheltenham. Wiggy was a great singer with a big voice, who sang in the typical Gypsy style: open, slow, and at considerable volume. Paul and I would have sessions with him either in his modest local, or else we would pick him up and drive him to other pubs in the area that tolerated live music. For all his rough ways, Wiggy took to us and was pleased to meet people who took a real pleasure in his songs. Apart from his family songs of old ballads, Irish ditties, plus songs of poaching and crime, he also sang songs he had learned from George Formby and Jimmie Rodgers records, as do many travellers.

Pete Wilson, a presenter on Radio Gloucestershire, was once interviewing me about recording Gypsy singers, and I told him about Wiggy and how he was happy for Paul and me to record him; but when other collectors came to try to record him, he told them to 'Go away'. Pete laughed and asked whether those were Wiggy's exact words. I replied, 'Not exactly, but it was the same number of words.'

One of my endearing memories is when Paul and I took Wiggy to the English Country Music Festival, where traditional singers encountered revival singers. Wiggy took centre-stage, even to the point of stopping one revival singer in mid-verse to tell him that he was not singing the song properly! He then went on to sing his version of the song. Imagine the singer's surprise. Fortunately, it was someone who knew Wiggy and was not offended. If a club singer had done this, they might have been lynched for the breach of etiquette, but Wiggy got away with it because everyone loved him. As time went on, Wiggy's health faded, and Paul and I attended his funeral in Cheltenham. In the pub afterwards, we sang some of his old songs in his memory.

A lack of tolerance towards Gypsies is manifest in the attitude of some of the good folk of the beautiful Cotswold market town of Stow-on-the-Wold, bristling with expensive antique shops, upmarket hotels, and chic coffee bars. Twice a year, Stow Horse Fair takes place, and it has a charter that goes back to the fifteenth century. Since the Second World War the fair has increasingly become a Gypsy fair and is now almost exclusively so. The fair is a riot of colour and movement as the Gypsies park their caravans, or 'trailers', as they usually call them, on the hillside at Maugersbury, adjacent to Stow. Then they set up stalls selling china, usually Crown Derby, linen, pots and pans, bric-a-brac, CDs and videos. The videos are of Gypsy life on the road, horses, shots of Appleby and Stow Fairs, and, amazingly, bare-knuckle fighting. When it rains at Stow Fair the whole thoroughfare between the stalls is a sea of mud, making progress hazardous. Gypsies, with the ladies dressed to the nines and often with gorgeous bare midriffs, stroll into town to see what is open and find some fish and chips for lunch. Meanwhile, on the field, families and friends socialise and swap gossip around open fires.

The impact on the town of Stow is that large parts of the town close for fear of the crimes the Gypsies might commit during fair week. All the pubs are shut, even those in nearby villages. That is not to say that Gypsies are blameless, but the disorder is probably no worse than what can be seen in a town centre on a Saturday night. The latter we encourage by condoning round-the-clock drinking, and the former we discourage by shutting up shop. I am not getting at the folks of Stow, as they must manage their town, but I am saying that the fair should be a joyous celebration of culture, not something that is dreaded. The Gypsies themselves have a duty to keep their act clean, but there is a need for a lot more tolerance and understanding on both sides.

It was not always so. Up until the mid-1990s the pubs did, in fact, stay open for Stow Fair, and sing-songs and step dancing were regular features in the bars. It may surprise readers to know that a Gypsy singaround is a very orderly affair. One person will sing at a time, usually a song rendered slowly with sobbing pathos, whilst the listeners give encouragement at the end of each verse with 'Go on, Joe' or 'Go on, gal'. By the mid-90s only a few pubs in Stow would let the Gypsies in, and then only if you knocked at the door and the landlord had a good look at you first through the peephole. I was lucky enough to be at one such singaround with Paul Burgess. After gaining admission, we were ushered into the back room, where there were a couple of dozen Gypsies. Paul and I regaled them with some lively fiddle and melodeon tunes, and eventually it was announced that Matt was going to sing. Matt Howard is a northerner who is a regular visitor to the fair and has a repertoire and singing style that would put most in the folk revival to shame.

Matt stood up and, having got the attention of the whole room, embarked on the tale of the greyhound 'Master McGrath', a story of an Irish greyhound matched against an English one. The story itself is true. Master McGrath was from County Waterford, owned and trained by one Lord Lurgan. On three occasions he was brought over to England for the Waterloo Cup, a hare-coursing race which today would be illegal. Master McGrath won the cup in 1868, 1869 and 1871, and became the most famous greyhound of his time. When 'The Master' died at the age of five, it was found that his heart was twice the normal size.

But back to Stow. Matt started the song and had the audience eating out of his hand:

> *In eighteen sixty-nine was the date of the year*
> *When the Waterloo sportsman with their dogs did appear*
> *That was the date England challenged the war*
> *With old Rose of old England……*

At this point, Matt stopped singing and growled at the listeners,

> *'Cos I'm a proper dog man!'*
> *……against the Master McGrath.*

Ten out of ten for presentation! In the song, Lord Lurgan lays a bet with the English:

> *Now Lord Lurgan stepped forward and he said, 'Gentlemen*
> *Is there one amongst you got money to spend?*
> *For you nobles of England I don't care a straw.*
> *There's five thousand I lay on my Master McGrath.'*

At the words 'money to spend', Matt pulled out a handful of loose change that he had been fondling in his pocket and tossed it on to the table in front of him with a grand gesture and a clatter and jingle of coins. More great presentation! As the song continued and the race between 'The Master' and 'Rose of Old England' progressed, the audience grew more excited, with even more cries of 'Go on, Matt', up until the final verse:

Now the hare she laid on just as swift as the wind
[rhymes with 'behind']
Old McGrath he passed Rosie, left Rosie behind
Jumped on the hare's back and he held up his old paw
Saying, 'The cup goes to Ireland and the Master McGrath.'

It was a masterly performance and one of the best renderings of a folk song that I have ever heard. Matt went on to sing about 'Appleby Fair', a similar Gypsy horse fair that takes place every year in Cumbria. The song started off as a poem written in 1954 by Harold Taylor and the language and imagery are very close to the heart of the travelling community:

There must have been trouble, cos in comes a cop
A man's had a scud [blow] *with an old kettle prop*
But nobody's manging [confessing], *'cos travellers don't talk*
Dick at him jelling [Look at him go], *he's halfway*

to York.

The song ends on an upbeat note:

From the highways and byways these travellers
have met
And it's win, lose, or draw, there'll be no regret
It's been a great pleasure to put them to verse
You'll often meet better, but oft times meet worse.

An old Gypsy skill, still seen from time to time, is step-dancing. The Gypsy step-dancers that I have come across have all excelled in their art, with a skill and showmanship that most of us can only envy. Step-dancing used to be common throughout these islands, mainly performed on Saturday nights in smoky bars on stone floors, by Gypsies and non-Gypsies alike. These days, the American-Irish, through the show *River Dance*, have taken step-dancing to the concert platform, but there are those in England who could rival Michael Flatley, given the chance. Anyone who has seen the Devon Gypsy Tommy Orchard dance can be in no doubt that they are witnessing a serious artiste perform.

In a Gloucestershire pub recently, I was lucky enough to see an expert local step-dancer, Bill Buckley. Encouraged by the music that my friends and I were playing and emboldened by the couple of dozen Gypsies who had come to cheer him on, he was asked to 'Give us a step, then, Bill'. This he did, with tremendous skill and presentation. On a recent trip to Andalusia I watched a Flamenco show. It was very professionally staged and performed, but as the show went on, I started to see parallels. The passionate *zapateado* or foot-tapping, the shouted cries of encouragement, even the appearance of the Gypsies with their dramatic looks and gestures, their sharp dress sense, and bold, weather-beaten features, took me right back to that Gloucestershire pub and 'Go on, Bill'.

But as the Gypsy way of life changes, so does its folklore. Step-dancers are fewer now, and ageing. There is still singing, but you are more likely to hear a cowboy song than an old English ballad these days. Once, when Wiggy Smith was singing in a pub in the presence of some other Gypsies, he performed with great style the poaching song that he called 'I Took My Dog', and which folklorists call 'When Gamekeepers Lie Sleeping'. This is a song that is often found in the repertoire of Gypsy singers:

> *I took that hare along the road*
> *And sold him for a crown-oh.*
> *They said they would give me a crown a brace*
> *If I could bring them fifty.*

Wiggy knew all about catching hares and selling them in pubs, so the song had a special resonance for him. At the end of the song, one of his fellow Gypsies said, 'That was very good, Wig, but now give us a *real old traveller song.* How about 'The Strawberry Roan'?' Now 'The Strawberry Roan' is an old cowboy song recorded by many, including Wiggy's hero Jimmie Rodgers. The irony that a twentieth-century cowboy song should be regarded as a 'real old traveller song', whilst an old English poaching song was not, was obviously lost on the speaker. But was he right? Wiggy's poaching song, admirable as it was, had clearly passed out of that listener's consciousness and was not part of his cultural experience, whereas 'The Strawberry Roan' was, as he had probably heard other Gypsies sing it numbers of times; and so, for him, yes, it was a 'real old traveller song'.

You can't stop cultural change, but change is not necessarily progress. It is, of course, a free world, and people are entitled to sing what they like. Should we lament that the old songs the Gypsies sang of love, drama, crime, and poaching are being replaced by American country and western songs? Well, perhaps we should. Freight trains, strawberry roans, and lonesome pines are really someone else's culture, not that of the English Gypsy. It is true that some English Gypsies, and some non-Gypsies who follow the traveller lifestyle, such as Mick and Pat Darling, are writing and performing songs about English Gypsy society, but they are rare animals.

About Gypsies and their right to respect, it is worth remembering two facts. The first is that Gypsies are a recognised ethnic group in the UK, and the second is that Gypsies were victims of the Holocaust. Fifteen thousand Gypsies died in Germany, three quarters of the Gypsy population. Where is their memorial?

Wiggy Smith – iconic Gypsy singer from Gloucestershire. Photo – Paul Burgess

Nightingales Sing – in the Appalachians

There was a period in the late 1990s when I had the opportunity to spend some time in the USA. I had been to the US for several short business trips, but had got no further than Washington, DC, so I jumped at the chance to spend a longer time there and to explore. Now, Washington is a great place, mainly because there are several folk there that know more about English folk song than most English folkies. Little did I expect to find, for example, a Jewish-American family whose music-making included a large chunk of the Copper family repertoire, or to meet people who knew more about the songs of Harry Cox than most people in an English folk club.

As I had spare time at the weekends, I decided to spend some of it seeking out source singers. The reaction of my new-found American friends was interesting, as they asked me what sort of American folk songs I wanted to hear. In fact, they presented me with a pick-list that included blues, gospel, shape-note singing, old timey, and even songs of Russian immigrants. After a moment's thought, I explained that I wanted to hear the sort of songs that relate to the English repertoire. That pub one evening, armed with melodeon and whistle, and regaling the locals in the bar with a couple of hours of tunes, interspersed with 'Who's going to give us a song, then?' Apart from boozy versions of 'Can you Rokka Romany?' and 'Mandi Went to Puv the Grai',[3] both songs in the Romany-inflected language that travellers use, and the Dubliners' version of 'Seven Nights Drunk', our efforts came to naught – until the very end of the evening, when one of the Gypsies came over to us and said in a hoarse voice that if we wanted to know about songs, he would lend us a book with all his family songs. Charlie went over to the campsite and came back with a home-produced, typewritten book entitled 'Songs and Ballads of the Brazil Family of Gloucester', with the words of fifty folk songs, each one a gem. That person with the hoarse voice was Danny Brazil.

Charlie and I carefully photocopied the book and returned it to Danny. I say carefully, as we did not want to incur the wrath of a traveller family by damaging or losing the book. Danny could not have been more co-operative, and when I returned the book to him a week later, he said, 'I suppose you want to know the tunes.' This was like asking the Pope if he was Catholic. The first song that Danny sang to me was 'The Banks of Sweet Dundee', and he rather confused me at first by announcing that Dundee was in Ireland. Danny's hoarse voice was apparently the result of a family fight some years beforehand, but if he had had his full voice,

---

[3] Literally, 'Can you speak Romany?' and 'I put the horse [*grai*] in the field [*puv*]', meaning that the Gypsy would let his horse graze, illegally, of course, overnight in a farmer's field.

when labour was needed for crop-picking, or buying and selling horses. Now the crops are picked by machine or by foreign labour and farm horses are a thing of the past. So, Gypsies have had to fall back on trades where they use their practical skills, such as scrap-metal dealing, tarmacing drives, or tree surgery. This has meant that Gypsies have been pushed further back to the fringes of society and are held accountable for all sorts of misdemeanours. 'Respectable' folk seem to forget that Gypsies do not hold a monopoly on bad behaviour. According to my observations, bad behaviour seems evenly distributed throughout society. I am a great believer in the idea that people treat you as you treat them. I have always treated Gypsies (and everyone else, I hope) with great respect, and have always been met with friendliness from them. However, I can see that if as a people you have been mistreated and despised over centuries, you are likely to build up an attitude and a hard exterior.

I gradually became aware, mainly through the recordings that Mike Yates had made for Topic Records, of the importance that English Gypsies have, or should it be had, for our traditions. I knew no local Gypsies, but was aware of a nearby pub, between Cheltenham and Gloucester, that was frequented by Gypsies, being located right outside an established Gypsy campsite. So, with my friend Charlie, himself an undiscovered traditional singer, we determined to do some research. This consisted of going along to the seemed to do the trick, and I was quickly put in touch with various folklorists in Virginia, West Virginia, and New York State. Unfortunately, North Carolina was just a touch too far, but it is still my ambition to sing in Ashville (not Nashville), as that area is a hotbed of Appalachian ballad singing.

At this point I realised something about American music that should have been blindingly obvious, which is just how *American* it is. To the American mind, there is a concept of music that is like a wheel with many spokes. One spoke is gospel, another jazz, another Cajun, another barbershop, another blues, another Tamla Motown, and so on, and the beauty of it is that all these strands are not only inter-related, but they are all American and blend into each other. So, an American can be equally proud of gospel or rock 'n' roll. Sure, other influences come into it, but they soon become assimilated, in the way that immigrants coming to Ellis Island a hundred years ago very soon became American. So, it is a truism that American music is just that – a hundred per cent American. It is instructive to compare this with the music we have in England. Do we have a similar wheel with spokes? Probably not. Of course, we have a very English sound in our folk music, church choirs, and brass bands, but these are mostly cul-de-sacs regarding any influence they might exert on the music put out by the media. At the risk of sounding like an old fogey, I can state that whereas music in the USA is one hundred per cent

American, music in England is only about ninety per cent American!

But I digress. My first effort at collecting was a trip down to Chilhowie, a modest town in the south of Virginia, just before it turns into North Carolina. The Virginia folklorist Roddy Moore, of Ferrum College, had recommended that I look up an old singer called Spencer Moore (presumably no relation). My attempts to talk to Spencer beforehand on the phone were hampered on both sides by problems understanding our respective accents, but nevertheless he understood what I wanted, and when I reached his house, he was ready and waiting, with his battered Gibson guitar in hand. I wasn't quite sure what to expect but having got used to the relative affluence of the residents of Washington, I was slightly surprised to see the modest nature of the housing in the rural areas of southern Virginia. Spencer's house was typical of the area: small and sparse.

Spencer greeted me like a long-lost friend and started singing me his songs before I could even get the tape recorder going. The revelation that he was a cousin of Dolly Parton was a surprise. I asked Spencer if he had met any English person before, and imagine my surprise when he responded that yes, he had been visited by Shirley Collins. In fact, unbeknown to me, he had been recorded by Alan Lomax and Shirley Collins in 1959. I was certainly following in some distinguished footsteps. I don't know how long Spencer had owned his guitar, but the worn-down frets and well-scratched fingerboard indicated that it had been the hero of many a hundred singing sessions. Despite his seventy-eight years, he flat-picked his guitar and sang his songs with a rare vigour. The jewel of his repertoire, at least to English folk-song collectors, is his version of 'The Wife of Usher's Well', a song that died out in England a century ago, but which still turns up regularly in the Appalachians. It is one of our beautiful supernatural ballads, a story of children dying but returning to their mother after death, before leaving her forever. Spencer's version is called 'Three Little Babes' and is a song he learned from his father:

There was a bride, a most beautiful bride
Three little babes had she
She sent them away to a northern college
To learn their grammaree.

They hadn't been away but a little while
'Bout three months and a day
Till death spread wide all over the land
And took her babes away.

Spencer's father had been a banjo-picker (Spencer used the old pronunciation, 'banjer'), and he picked his guitar almost like a banjo player. However, his guitar treatment using the three-chord trick sometimes obscured the modal character of the tune – a small niggle considering that I was hearing a song preserved in direct oral tradition that had been lost in England a hundred years ago. Song after song followed, including his lively version of 'The Devil and the Farmer's Wife' and the haunting 'Girl I Left Behind Me' (not the 'Brighton Camp' version, but a different song entirely).

Spencer Moore – veteran folk singer from Virginia in 1997.
Photo – Gwilym Davies

Spencer kept me entertained for a Saturday and a good part of Sunday morning before I had to set off back to Washington, DC. A bonus was that a lady neighbour called in on him while I was there and proceeded to demonstrate the local version of step-dancing, which she called 'flat-footing'. Spencer's guitar accompaniments fitted the dance perfectly.

On the way back, I had arranged to call in on Jim Marshall, another singer and mean bluegrass banjo-picker. Jim had assembled a group of singers and musicians for me that day and they spent the afternoon making music in his large bric-a-brac warehouse, but Murphy's law decreed that my temperamental DAT recorder went on the blink that day. I sat there in simmering frustration as Jim and his friends played tune after tune and sang song after song, including a brilliant version of 'The Mermaid', which I shall never hear again.

That was my only collecting trip to Virginia, but a memorable one, not least for the three-hundred-mile trip back to Maryland, on Route 81, in the lashing rain and spray, when all I could see in the rear-view mirror was the radiator of a large and powerful American truck travelling at about 75mph ten yards behind me. One slip on my part and I would have been roadkill.

My other Appalachian collecting trips were thanks to Gerry Milnes of the Augusta Heritage Center in Elkins, West Virginia. Any Englishman going to the Center should salivate with jealousy that we do not have an equivalent institute in England. It is a residential college that runs courses and workshops, organises folk events, does collecting, and has a substantial archive, mainly of local West Virginia music. All this is in a humble town of just over seven thousand inhabitants. Imagine such a thing in an English town of the same size.

Roddy Moore had put me in touch with a local singer, Helena Triplett, a lady who originally hails from New Zealand, as can be heard when she speaks. But when she sings or plays the banjo, she is the authentic Appalachian performer. She has embraced and learned the style and is regarded as one of the top interpreters of folk song in the area. Helena was pleased to join me in my collecting trip to Glenville, West Virginia, where we were warmly welcomed by the seventy-four-year-old Phyllis Marks at her modest trailer home. Phyllis has been blind for about fifteen years but remains fiercely independent.

Phyllis is an impressive woman in many ways. Her memory for old songs and her delight in singing them is so evident. It seemed that every time I asked her for a song, she had a version of it:

'Phyllis, do you know "Barbara Allen"?'

'Sure do.'

'Could you sing it for me?'

'Okay.'

And so on for 'The Two Sisters', 'Lord Thomas and Fair Eleanor', 'The House Carpenter', 'Lord

Lovell', and so forth. Folk-song collecting with Phyllis Marks was like holding a jug under a waterfall. I was particularly pleased to record 'Lord Lovell', as my wife Carol has been known to sing a version of the song collected in our home county of Gloucestershire. It was even sung to a similar tune.

At this point I tried to imagine the thoughts of the pioneer folk-song collectors, Cecil Sharp and Maud Karpeles, as they travelled around the Appalachians by foot, mule, and horse eighty years before. I had looked at Sharp's Appalachian manuscripts at Clare College, Cambridge, where he had studied, and noticed that singer after singer in the Appalachians in those years had sung 'The House Carpenter' and 'Lord Lovell' for Cecil and Maud. I suppose that after you have heard the first thirty renderings of each, your eyes might glaze over. I had a wicked mental picture of them spending a day slogging up to a remote mountain top to find an old singer, who then greeted them with 'I'm going to sing you good folks two songs that my pappy taught me. You might not know these songs; one is called "House Carpenter" and the other "Lord Lovell".' At this point, Cecil might have forced a smile, coupled with a sigh, given Maud a weary glance, and said, 'Wonderful. I would love to hear those songs.'

Phyllis bears her blindness lightly and is an icon amongst West Virginian traditional singers. She sang me, without the slightest tinge of irony, the old story of the woman who makes her husband blind by feeding him marrowbones:

Gwilym recording the blind ballad singer, Phyllis Marks, from West Virginia in 1998.Photo – Gwilym Davies

There was a lady gay and, in our town, did dwell
She loved her husband dearly and another one twice as well
Chorus: *Mush-em tiggery awri awri*
Mush-em tiggery awri-ay.

She listened at the keyhole, she heard the old man say
'If I suck six dozen marrybones, it'll take my sight away.'
She ran to the butcher to see what she could find
She got six dozen marrybones to make the old man blind.

The husband wickedly gets his revenge by drowning her:

She got upon the brink to push the old man in
He stuck out his feet and she went thrashing in.

'It's murder, it's murder,' as loud as she could scream
'I'd help you,' said the old man, 'But I cannot see a thing.'

He being kind-hearted, he knew she couldn't swim
He went and got a long pole and pushed her further in.

Phyllis's last verse is one I had never come across before, when the husband sadly proclaims:

I have eleven children and none of them are mine
I wish that every country gent would come and claim his own.

That being the case, it does indeed give a motive for his unwillingness to prevent his wife drowning. What a wicked woman!

For a time, Helena and I sat on the porch of Phyllis's trailer, listening to and recording her old ballads. By us sat Phyllis's beautiful golden Labrador guide dog, Sally, who slept on, probably dreaming of chasing rabbits. In about verse three of Phyllis's version of 'Hear the Nightingale Sing', Sally awoke with the loudest sneeze I have ever heard from a dog. The recording session stopped abruptly with gales of laughter from Helena, Phyllis, and me, and a puzzled expression from Sally, as much as to say, 'What...?'

Still chuckling, Phyllis said, 'I guess you'd like me to start that song again.'

A YouTube video from 2016 shows Phyllis still singing her old ballads with impressive vigour at the age of eighty-nine.

Phyllis and Helena accompanied me to visit another West Virginia ballad singer, ninety-year-old Rita Emerson in Glenville, Gilmore County. She pronounced her first name to sound like 'Rider' to my English ears. As Phyllis and Rita were old friends, conversation and songs flowed, including another version of 'Lord Lovell', which she claimed was an English song that she had learnt from her father. Rita also knew several 'play-party' songs, which were really children's singing games, but she said that they were not allowed to dance when she was a child, however play-party games were fine. Thus, Rita sang and then described the games of 'King William', 'There Goes a Red Bird through the Window', 'Skip to my Lou', 'Two Young Couples Went Skating Away', 'Weevily Wheat', and 'Old Dusty Miller', games that have long been lost on this side of the Atlantic.

Helena and I had many long chats about folk song during that collecting trip, discussing our various views, and exploding my notion that Americans don't sing bawdy songs. They certainly do; but, apart from a few specialist collections, they don't appear in print. Helena certainly knew the odd ditty collected locally that your maiden aunt would not approve of. I would guess that Phyllis knew quite a few songs that she would not dream of singing to collectors. However, that was not the case with the brilliant Cleveland family of New York State.

Paint It Green – in the Adirondacks

When New York is mentioned, most people think of the city. In fact, the city of New York, although accounting for forty per cent of the population of New York State, only accounts for about seven per cent of the total area. This means that outside the city of New York, the population density is very thin, so that 'neighbours' can mean anyone within a hundred-mile radius, and people will think nothing of driving long distances to call in on friends. In other words, apart from a few centres of urbanisation such as Albany, Rochester, Yonkers, and Buffalo, New York State is mainly empty. Running through the state are the beautiful Adirondack Mountains, which are not all snowy towering peaks like the Rocky Mountains, but rather gentle wooded slopes and valleys. Also, New York State reaches as far as the Canadian border, which means that in winter it can be seriously cold. Ice storms are not infrequent.

There are pockets of Native American culture there, namely Mohawk and Iroquois, with their own traditions. In this emptiness, immigrants from Ireland and elsewhere came in large numbers and settled. The traditions and folk music of the state are distinctive and echo the old world in surprising ways. Here you will find a storyteller with old European folk tales, and there a fiddler with a style not far removed from many traditional Scottish or Irish players. Amongst the singers and their repertoire, you will find constant echoes of the British Isles, from ballads long forgotten on this side of the pond to a singing style that would not sound out of place in a Devon pub. On top of this, you have the locally composed songs which tell tales of lumberjacks and... well, mainly of lumberjacks, actually.

Friends in DC had recommended to me on several occasions that I should meet Colleen Cleveland and the Cleveland family from the Adirondacks, and I had the opportunity to meet Colleen and her seventeen-year-old nephew at the Connecticut Folk Festival in 1997. I was more used to English folk festivals than American ones, so my query as to where the bar was met with uncomprehending blank looks. I was told that there was a Coca-Cola machine, but sorry, no bar. That was a great culture shock to me, as nearly all my musical experiences in England had been conducted within sight of a pint. By the same token, there was a dearth of melodeons. So, a folk festival with no beer and no melodeons? However, I readjusted to this and carried on. Colleen had travelled down for the festival from her home in the Brant Lake area with her nephew James. She told me how her grandmother, the great American ballad singer Sara Cleveland, had been discovered by the folk world when Sara's son Jim had written down some of the words of the songs and taken them along to the old-established Saratoga Springs folk club in New York State. The club residents at first did not believe Jim and thought it unlikely that his mother, living in a totally remote part of the state, should know such rare songs. However, it dawned on them that a rare source of folk songs had been discovered, and so collectors like Kenneth Goldstein and Sandy Paton went to visit Sara. It transpired that Sara, of Irish origin, knew about two hundred songs, many of them to glorious tunes, including the rare 'Queen Jane', the only transatlantic version of rare Child ballad 'The King's Dochter Lady Jean', an incest ballad that had died out in the British Isles many decades previously. Sara soon became known to larger audiences and easily transferred her songs from the country kitchen to the folk festival circuit.

Colleen spoke warmly of her grandmother and said that Sara sang just as easily and confidently to the large festival audiences as she had in the family home, and audiences warmed to her and her wicked sense of humour. One of her party pieces at home, which was always the last song the Cleveland children wanted her to sing before they went to sleep, was the gloriously bawdy song with the refrain:

Rumshe-idity, rum she-i
Rumshe-idity, rum she-i
Rumshe-idity, rum she-i

And the old woman shit in the corner.

Apparently, Sara was not afraid to sing this at folk festivals, including Newport. I love the idea of an audience of ten thousand bawling out the chorus.

While Sara was being fêted by the folk community in the 1960s, there was a little girl at her side quietly absorbing all the songs. That was, of course, Colleen, who grew up hearing Sara's ballads of incest, death, destruction, piracy, bawdiness, and unrequited love. What a superb education! It soon dawned on Colleen that she had a wonderful singing voice, and since Sara's death in 1992 she has been a champion of her family songs. At the same time, she has kept her feet firmly on the ground in her community and has held several jobs, such as decorating and acting as a forest guide. Imagine the reaction of her colleagues as she sings old ballads while slapping on the paint. Colleen and I got on very well from the start and she agreed at that festival in Connecticut to let me record her singing a couple of her grandmother's songs, starting with the famous 'Queen Jane':

Queen Jane sat at her window one day
Sewing a silken seam
She looked out the merry green wood
And saw the green nut tree
And saw the green nut tree.

Colleen Cleveland and her nephew, James – traditional singers
from New York State, 1998,
Photo – Gwilym Davies

In fact, the only place we could find to record in the school where the folk festival was being held was in a lobby area, surrounded by glass doors. The resulting recording therefore has a nice echo sound to it, and what a song! Colleen introduced me to her nephew James, a surprisingly mature seventeen-year-old who was getting into the family repertoire and who sings with natural charm.

After that brief encounter in Connecticut, I determined to make a trip up to see more of the Cleveland family, which I did, mainly thanks to George and Vaughn Ward of Albany. George and Vaughn welcomed me into their home and arranged for me to meet a procession of singers and storytellers, including Dick Richards, Catherine LaBier and the wonderful

Cleveland family. I kept in touch with George and Vaughn for several years afterwards, but Vaughn sadly died of cancer in 2001.

We in England tend to think of America as being a highly populated country, but it is not so. Many Americans live in remote areas and the Cleveland family are no exception. Colleen's parents, Jim and Phyllis, lived in a house on the edge of the woods, with the next house, owned by Colleen's brother, about half a mile away. It was an idyllic scene for a folk-song collector, surrounded by forest and mountains, with the January snow on the ground. Even though the temperature scarcely rose above freezing, there was an abundance of wildlife frequenting the bird feeders outside the kitchen window. I sat there transfixed as a succession of squirrels, blue jays, chickadees, and various shades of woodpecker paraded before my eyes. Jim Cleveland, Colleen's father, had not long left hospital and was not in the best of health, but was very willing to go through Sara's collection of words of songs and sing us what tunes he could remember, encouraged by young James, who was keen to find out as much as he could about the family songs. We had to compete with some very loud caged birds in the family kitchen, not to mention a central heating system that came on from time to time with loud clicks, roars, and rumbles.

When I came to record Colleen, I mentioned these various audible obstacles to getting a clean recording and she suggested we record on the outside porch. Now remember that this was in January in an area not too far from Canada. The hardy Clevelands were used to it, but not a soft English townie. When the ice started to thaw on the puddles by about three in the afternoon, they declared that it was, 'Pretty nice out today.' Anyway, once Colleen and I had got installed on the porch, away from birds and central heating, we were ready. Colleen started to sing her version of 'Scarborough Fair'. And then the chainsaw started up… You would think that in such a remote area it would be quite easy to get away from extraneous noises, but no. The sound of a chainsaw carries an impressive distance in the cold still days of an Adirondack winter and certainly was not wanted on my recording. Colleen and I just had to wait for breaks in the logging activities to record the songs, and then get back to the warmth of the kitchen.

I was also fascinated by the fact that Colleen had learned several folk-tales from her grandmother. I knew a little about the Jack tales of the Appalachians, but the Clevelands had Tim tales. Tim the Irishman was usually the hero, outwitting giants and devils with equal ease. One story that Colleen told me brings together ancient folk motifs, pride in Irish ancestry, and the Cleveland family's wicked sense of humour:

'There were three men walking down the road in Ireland one day, travelling about their way, and as they were going down the road, out from behind the bushes

jumps the Devil and he stops them, and he says, "I'm going to whisk you all away to hell." They obviously didn't want to go, so they complained, and he said, "All right, I'll make you a deal. If each one of you can set me a task that I can't do, then you get to go free."

So, the Englishman steps up first and he looks off in the distance and there was a big huge mountain. He looks at the Devil and says, "Here, you make that mountain disappear," and the Devil smiles and goes whoosh... and away goes the mountain. And whoosh... away goes the Englishman.

Well, that was that and the Scotsman was next, and he looks off into the distance and there's a big huge lake and he says, "Well, make the lake disappear all in a minute." And the Devil looks at him and whoosh... away goes the lake. Again whoosh... and away goes the Scotsman.

And the Irishman stands there and he thinks and he thinks and he looks at the Devil and all of a sudden he lets out a great big huge fart and he says, "Catch that, bottle it, and paint it green all in a minute," and you know the Devil he couldn't and he had to let him go.'

Of all the singers I met in America in 1997 and 1998, it was Colleen that impressed me most. She was certainly the most accomplished singer that I met during that time, but I was also struck by her commitment to the family tradition, whilst at the same time keeping that earthiness that is the essence of true folk song. However, all the performers I met were remarkable in many ways. For instance, there was Catherine LaBier, who, although well into her sixties, drove seventy miles to meet me in Albany and let me record her amazing stories of the Adirondacks, with ghostly fiddlers, talking bones, and shape-shifting wolves. Catherine's ancestors were of French stock, and whilst some of her stories were local folk-tales, such as 'How bears got into the Adirondacks' or 'How the Beluga whale became white', others were of more European origin, harking back many centuries. Here is her story of 'The Singing Bones', which, whilst some of the language has French overtones, goes straight back to European equivalents, often known as 'The Story of Orange'. Scottish Gypsies have a version of this tale. In Catherine's story, a boy and a girl were sent by their mother to collect wood for the oven. The girl collected wood, but the boy spent all the time playing with a bird that insisted on flying around him. When they returned home, the mother was angry with the boy, and while he was raiding the biscuit barrel, she chopped off his head and then proceeded to cook him. The story continues:

'It was almost dinner time and Papa was coming home and he could smell something good cooking. And when he got into the house he says, "Woman," he says, "where did you get the meat? I could find nothing out in the woods today." And, well, she says, "A neighbour came in and gave us some meat." And he says, "Well, it smells good," he says, "and I'm starved. Feed me." And he called the little girl, but she got under the table and little tears were coming down her eyes, and he says, "Get up here and eat with us." And she says, "No, I just want the bones," she says, "and I'll gather them in my little handkerchief." Well, they started to eat, and he was giving her the bones under the table when along came this bird. And the little bird was singing:

"My mother cooked me, my father did eat me,
And my sister will gather my tiny little bones in her handkerchief."

Well, Mama was very upset about this, so she kicked the little girl and she says, "Get out there and chase that bird away!" So, the little girl did. She got up and she took the broom and she chased the little bird into the woods.

Well, a short time later she came out of the woods and walked into the house and she had on a brand-new dress with a beautiful ribbon sash and a big bow to match in her hair and new shoes on her feet. Mama

said, "Where did you get those new things from?"
She says, "The little bird gave them to me." She says,
"Hmmph! Likely story!" But the little girl got back
under the table and spread out her handkerchief and
started to gather once again Papa's bones. Well, a
short time later that little bird came back and singing
the same little song: .

"My mother will cook me, my father will eat me,
And my sister will gather my tiny little bones in
her handkerchief."

Well, Mama was really upset, and she said to
Papa, "Take that broom and go on and get rid of that
bird once and for all!"
So, he went outside and he's chasing the bird into
the woods and a short time later he came out and he
had a brand-new suit, new boots, even a gold fob on
his waistcoat, and a new chapeau. And Mama said,
"Where did you get those new things from?" And he
says, "That bird gave 'em to me." She said, "Likely
story!" So, they finished up dinner and they were
enjoying it and the little girl was still under the table
gathering those tiny little bones when that bird came
back, and Mama says, "I will take care of that bird this
time." So, she picked out the broom and the little bird
had perched on the porch roof and she went out and she
started to hit that little bird and the sky really darkened
and the thunder roared. And a streak of lightning came

*down and struck Mama into a pile of dust. And the
wind gusted up and blew open the door and blew all
the dust into the house. And that, my friends, is why we
have dust in our house.'*

Then there was Dick 'Daddy' Richards, who,
despite losing his left hand in a paper-mill accident
when quite young, re-learned how to play the fiddle
and guitar. At the age of nearly eighty, he was still
running a local dance band. His version of 'The Devil
and the Farmer's Wife' is a recording that I greatly
treasure. Dick's grand-daughter, Heather Richards,
is now a professional songwriter and singer, so the
musical tradition of the family is being continued.

It was Daddy Richards who made me an honorary
member of the Adirondack Liars Club. Why I was
made a member of the Liars Club I don't know, but
I felt it was a great honour. When I recounted this
in a talk I gave back in England, a member of the
audience asked how they could know I was telling
the truth. The tradition of meeting to tell tall tales is

known in many parts of the English-speaking world. The winner for the evening is the one who can tell the tallest and most entertaining story. The same tales turn up in places as far apart as Devon and North Carolina, where, for example, a hunter bends the barrel of his rifle and with one shot, which naturally goes around in a circle, manages to kill many game birds, rabbits and sundry other animals for the pot. In the North Carolina version, the hunter is standing in a river at the time and arrives home to find his boots full of trout. Jim Cleveland had many such tales. Here is one:

'Fishbrook Pond is on the east side of Lake George over here. It's on the top of Sleeping Beauty Mountain. I climbed up on top of there – good for trout. Well, I was going up there fishing, you know, quite a long hike up to the top of it. And I got a pretty good string of fish and I figured I'd better head back. I started down and I got pretty near to the end and these Coy dogs or Coyotes, I don't know what you call them. Anyway, there was a bunch of them got after me. So, I threw the fish down. They got that, and I climbed a tree. Well, I was up in the tree there a while and I thought that when they got tired, they'd go, you know, and I wasn't too far from where I had the truck parked. So, they kept circling round there, sat around and pretty soon the biggest one, I thought he was the boss, he took off and went up the hill; you know. I figured, Jeez, the rest of them would go. Pretty soon, about five minutes, he came back, and he was leading a beaver to cut down the goddamn tree for them, so they could get at me.'

A likely story.

Comparisons are always odious, but I found in America a freshness of attitude towards their traditional music that is not always evident on this side of the Atlantic. As a generalisation, Americans are confident of their heritage and take pride in it. Of course, there is a great gap between the pop and folk worlds, but both parties respect each other's music as part of the great American picture. Because there is a certain esteem in performing and preserving American vernacular culture, public funds are more readily available, and so centres (or should I say 'centers') of excellence are established, such as the Augusta Heritage Center or the American Folklife Center at the Library of Congress, with its huge collection of field recordings. Our equivalent in England is the British Library Sound Archive, which, despite its role as a national centre for our folk-song recordings, has no one on the staff who is an expert on English folk music, so our folk music is just one slice of their World and Traditional Music section, competing for funding with music from a host of other cultures. This is, of course, symptomatic of the low esteem in which English folk music is held by the powers-that-be. It is part of a continuing attitude that denies that England has a viable folk culture. However, ask the thousands of people who each year attend folk festivals, sing and play in pub sessions, or don Morris kit whether they consider there is a folk culture or not.

Postscript

My audio recordings of source singers recorded from 1970 onwards will be available in 2020 to the public via the British Library Sound Archive website. The recordings are a 'warts and all' collection, but it contains some real gems, not only big ballads, but music-hall songs, drinking songs, navy ditties, wassails, children's rhymes, stories, step-dance tunes, and so on. Each song will have meant something to somebody at one time, in the sense that they took the pains to learn it. The collection is different in kind to the sort of things that older collectors found, reflecting a different era and considering that time, culture, human perceptions, and tastes in music all move on. So, many of the items are probably such that collectors like Sharp would have disdained. Nevertheless, it does represent a snapshot of culture at a time and place, and as such I hope that many will find their own jewels in listening to the recordings.

The music online is not the totality of my collecting. There remains a good deal of video, particularly of Gypsy performers, that is still in my private archive. I hope that one day these will be made available for all to see as well.

Appendix – Collected Songs

The following transcriptions give the bare bones of many of the songs mentioned in the book. However, a mere paper transcription cannot convey the subtleties of timing and expression that go into a performance. Most of these can be heard eventually on the British Library Sounds website, except for numbers 2 and 3, which are from the Davies family oral tradition.

APPENDIX OF SONGS AND TUNES

Andrew Bergine

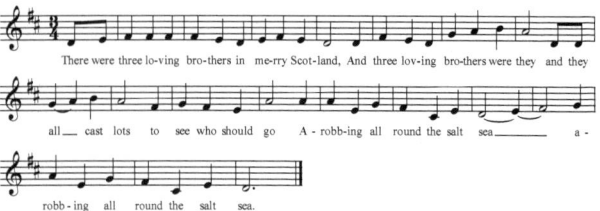

There were three lo-ving bro-thers in me-rry Scot-land, And three lov-ing bro-thers were they and they all — cast lots to see who should go A - robb-ing all round the salt sea — a - robb - ing all round the salt sea.

1. There were three loving brothers in Merry Scotland
And three loving brothers were they
And they all cast lots to see who should go
A-robbing all round the salt sea,
A-robbing all round the salt sea.

2. The lot it fell to Andrew Bergine
The youngest one of the three
That he should go sailing all round the salt sea
To keep his two brothers and he,
To keep his two brothers and he.

3. He sail-ed east, he sail-ed west
Until three ships he espied
A-sailing far off and a-sailing far on
'Til at last they came sailing close by,
'Til at last they came sailing close by.

4. "Who's there, who's there?" cried Andrew Bergine
"Who's there with colours so high?"
"We are three merchant ships from merry England.
And if no offence, let us pass by,
And if no offence, let us pass by."

5. "Oh no, oh no," cried Andrew Bergine
"Oh no, that never can be.
For your ships and your cargo my men they will have,

And your bodies I'll sink in the sea,
And your bodies I'll sink in the sea."

6. So broadside to broadside the vessels did sail
And cannons so loudly did roar.
And Andrew Bergine sank the three merchant ships
And he sailed off to find some more,
And he sailed off to find some more.

7. Then the news it reached King Henry's ear
The king that sat on the throne
That his ships and his cargo at sea were all lost
And his merry men they were all drowned,
And his merry men they were all drowned.

8. The king, he sent for Captain Charles Stuart
Saying "This thing you must do for me.
Go build you a ship and catch Andrew Bergine
And his body you'll sink in the sea,
And his body you'll sink in the sea."

9. The ship it was built and ready to sail
With cannons and men by the score
And one dark morning her anchor did weigh
And she sailed from old England's shore,
And she sailed from old England's shore.

10. She sail-ed east, she sail-ed west
Until three ships she espied
A-sailing far off and a-sailing far on
'Til at last they came sailing close by,
'Til at last they came sailing close by.

11. "Who's there, who's there?" cried Captain
Charles Stuart.
"Who's there with colours so high?"

"We are three bold robbers from merry Scotland.
And if no offence, let us pass by,
And if no offence, let us pass by."

12. "Oh, no, oh no" cried Captain Charles Stuart
"Oh no, that never can be.
For your ships and your cargo my men they will have,
And your bodies I'll sink in the sea,
And your bodies I'll sink in the sea."

13. So broadside to broadside the vessels did sail
And cannons so loudly did roar.
And Andrew Bergine beat Captain Charles Stuart
And he sent him back to England's shore,
And he sent him back to England's shore.

14. "Go back, go back," said Andrew Bergine
"And tell old King Henry for me
That he may be king of all England,
But I will reign over the sea,
But I will reign over the sea."

This epic song was sung to me by Colleen Cleveland of Brant Lake, New York State, USA, in 1998. Colleen had learnt the song from her grandmother, Sara. The song itself exists in various versions in the USA and Canada and gave rise to the English Song 'Henry Martin'.

The song is based on history: Andrew Barton (c. 1466-1511) was a Scottish sailor who, around the year 1507, was commissioned by James IV of Scotland to attack Portuguese ships who had attacked Scottish ships. His interference with Portuguese shipping earned him the reputation in England of being a pirate. In 1511, Barton was captured off Kent. Balladry has it that Barton was subsequently beheaded, despite his letter of permission from the Scottish king, although another account states that he died as a result of wounds sustained from the battle.

So you can't rely on folk songs to recount history accurately.

Around Her Leg She Wore a Yellow Garter

1. Around her leg she wore a yellow garter
She wore it in the springtime and in the month of May
(hey, hey)
And if you ask her why the hell she wore it
She wore it for that airman who is far, far away
Far far away (not far enough), far away (not far
enough)
She wore it for that airman who is far, far away.

2. And in the spring she wheels a perambulator
She wheels it in the springtime and in the month of
May (hey, hey)
And if you ask her why the hell she wheels it
She wheels it for that airman who is far, far away.
Far away etc.

3. Behind the door her father keeps a shotgun
He keeps it in the springtime and in the month of May
(hey, hey)
And if you ask him why the hell he keeps it
He keeps it for that airman who is far, far away.
Far away etc.

This song is one of many I learnt out of the earshot of the teachers at my secondary school in the early 60s. We had a body of songs, mainly bawdy. This is one of the cleaner ones.

Down by the Bramble Bushes

Down by the bramble bushes, down by the sea (clap, clap, clap)
True love for you, my darling, true love for me.
When we get married, we'll raise a family.

Spoken:
A boy for you, a girl for me
How many fishes in the sea?
Twelve and twelve make twenty-four
Kick your teacher out the door.
If she does not understand that
Hit her on the head with a baseball bat.
Teacher, teacher, I declare
I can see your underwear.
Is it black or is it white?
Oh my gosh, it's dynamite.
10, 9, 8, 7, 6, 5, 4, 3, 2, 1.
Blast off!

I have always had a fascination for playground rhymes and used my daughter as a collector when she was about seven years old. This is one of the delightful rhymes that she came back with.

Jan's Courtship

1."Come lis-ten son Jan, now__ thou art a man, I'll give thee best coun-sel in life__ . Come

sit down by me and my sto-ry shall be, I'll tell how to get thee a wife, Yes I will man I

will, sure I will, and I'll tell how to get thee a wife."__

[*Variant - last verse]

soon-er stay sin-gle the whole of my life

1. "Come listen son Jan, now thou art a man,
I'll give thee best counsel in life.
Come sit down by me and my story shall be
I'll tell how to get thee a wife,
Yes I will, man I will, sure I will
And I'll tell how to get thee a wife."

2. "Thyself thee must dress in thy Sunday go best,
They'll first turn away and be shy.
But boldly thou kiss each pretty maid that thou see'st
They'll call thee their love by and by
Yes they will, man they will, sure they will
And they'll call thee their love by and by."

3. So a-courting Jan goes, in his Sunday best clothes,
All trimmed, nothing tattered nor torn.
From the top to the toe with a bright yellow rose,
He looked like a gentleman born
Yes 'e did, man 'e did, sure 'e did
And he looked like a gentleman born.

4. The first pretty lass that Jan did see pass
Was a farmer's fat daughter named Grace.
He'd scarce said "How do?" and a fine word or two,

When her fetched him a slap in the face
Yes, 'er did, man 'er did, sure 'er did
And 'er fetched him a slap in the face.

5. Now Jan never caring of nothing at all
Was a-walking one day by the lock.
He kissed parson's wife, which caused such a strife,
And Jan was put in to the stocks
Yes he was, man he was, sure he was
And Jan was put into the stocks.

6. "If this be the way to get me a wife,"
Thinks Jan, "then I'll never have none.
I'd sooner stop single the whole of me life,
And home to me mammy I'll run
Yes I will, man I will, sure I will
And home to me mammy I will.

*This was one of the first songs that our neighbour,
Archer Goode, sang to Carol and me in 1975. He
learnt it from Sam Bennett, an old Morris dancer from
Ilmington in Warwickshire.*

Jimmie Cooper's Stepdances

In 1979, my wife and I attended the very first Dartmoor Folk Festival and were delighted to witness the stepdance display on the back of a farm wagon, with Bob Cann acting as MC and Jimmie Cooper playing the concertina. We recorded these two lively stepdance tunes from Jimmie. The first is well-known among Devon musicians. The second tune, Jack the Lad, is a variant of what Bob Cann called Cokie's Hornpipe.

John Barleycorn

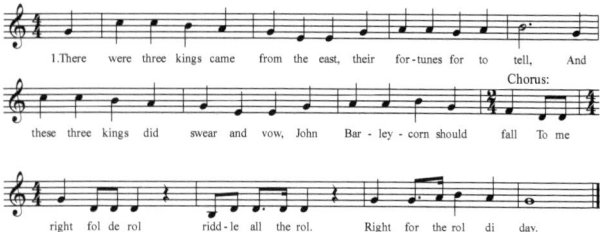

1. There were three kings came from the east,
   their fortunes for to tell.
And these three kings did swear and vow,
   John Barleycorn should fall.

Chorus: To me right fol de rol, riddle all the rol.
   Right fol the rol di day.

2. They got their ploughs, they ploughed him in,
   put clods all over his head,
And these three kings did swear and vow,
   John Barleycorn was dead.

3. John he laid in the ground for one fortnight,
   the rain from Heaven did send,
John Barleycorn sprang up his head,
   made liars of them all.

[4. There he remained 'til midsummer,
   and looked both pale and wan,
Then Barleycorn he got a beard
   and so became a man.]
5. The farmer with his scythe so sharp,
   he cut him off at knee
[And then poor little Barleycorn
   they used most barbarously.]

6. The pitcher with his pronged hook sharp,
   he stabbed him through the heart
[And like a dreadful tragedy,
   they bound him to a cart.]

[7. They hired men with crab-tree sticks
   who cut him skin from bone,
The miller served him worse than that
   and ground him 'twixt two stones.]

8. Here's brandy in a bottle
   and cider in a can,
But Barleycorn in a stout pint mug
   will floor the jolliest man.

This song has a special place in my affections as it is the first real folk song that I collected, from Charlie Milam of Long Sutton, Hampshire, in 1970. Charlie was born towards the end of the nineteenth century and had been a carter all his working life. He could not remember all the words, so I have supplied some [between brackets] from other versions.

Lamkin

1. Oh the lord said to his lady before he went out
"Beware of Long Lamkin for he's walking about."

2. "What care I for Long Lamkin or any of his kin,
When the doors they are all bolted and the windows
close pinned?"

3. One door left unbolted, Long Lamkin crept in
For to prick that little baby with a silver bodkin.

4. Said Lamkin to the false nurse, "Where's the heir
of this house?"
"He's asleep in his cradle as quiet as a mouse."

5. How sound he does slumber, how sound he does
sleep.
Then with a silver bodkin stabbed the baby so deep.

6. "Oh lady, oh lady, how sound does he sleep.
Don't you hear your little baby for to mourn and to
weep."
"How durst I come down in the midst of the night
No candle a-burning, or fire alight."

7. "Put on your gold mantle, you may see by that."
Bold Lamkin, he was ready for to catch her in his lap.

8. "Oh Lamkin, oh Lamkin, spare my life one half hour
I'll fetch you my daughter Betsy, she's the sweetest of flower."

9. "What care I for your daughter Betsy or any of your kin?
She may hold the silver basin for to catch your blood in."

10. There's blood in the kitchen, there's blood in the hall.
There's blood in the parlour where the lady did fall.

11. 'Twas early next morning before break of day
When the maid saw her master come a-riding that way
"Oh master, oh master, don't you lay the blame onto me
Bold Lamkin he has murdered the lady and the baby."

12. Bold Lamkin shall be hung from the gallows so high
And the false nurse shall be burned in the fire close by.
The bells will ring slowly, they'll make a dull sound
With the lady and the baby lay dead on the ground.

This gory and dramatic ballad has been around for at least 250 years. Despite its grim plot, it has persisted in oral tradition until recent times. I recorded this version from Tony Lloyd of Malvern in 1993. He learnt it from a local Gypsy singer.

Lemmie's Hornpipes

"Irish Hornpipe"

"Tap Dance, the other Irish Hornpipe"

Lementina Brazil, known to her family as Lemmie, played melodeon tunes that she had learnt in England and Ireland and often played for step dancing. The second of these tunes was picked up by the folk revival as Lemmie's Number 2 and is often played in tune sessions. I recorded her first in 1977.

My Bonny Bon Boy

1. "What had you for your dinner, my bonny, bon boy?
What had you for your dinner, my comfort and joy?
"Oh, eels boiled in butter, mother, make my bed soon
For I'm sick unto my heart and I want to lie down."

2. "What will you leave your brother," etc
"Oh, my horse and my saddle," etc

3. "What will you leave your father," etc
"Oh, my house and my lands," etc

4. "What will you leave your mother," etc
"Oh, the gates to heaven open," etc

5. "What will you leave your wife," etc
"Oh, the gates to hell wide open," etc

This unusual version of Lord Randal has been sung in the Cleveland family for generations and I was delighted to record 17 year old James Cleveland continuing the family tradition when I went to visit the family in New York State in January 1998.

Wassail Song (Shurdington)

1. Here we come a-wass'ling all over the town,
Our cup it is white and our ale it is brown.
Our bowl it is made of the sycamore tree
To my waysailing bowl I'll drink unto thee.

2. Here's to the (h)ox and to his right horn
God send my master a good crop of corn.
A good crop of corn that we may all taste
To my waysailing bowl, don't drink it in haste.

3. Here's to the (h)ox and to his right ear,
God send my master a barrel of beer.
A barrel of beer that we may all taste
To my waysailing bowl, don't drink it in haste.

4. Here's to the (h)ox and to his right eye
God send my master a good Christmas pie
A good Christmas pie that we may all taste
To my waysailing bowl, don't drink it in haste.

5. Here's to the (h)ox and to his right leg
Wishing my master a barrel of keg.
A barrel of beer that we may all taste
To my waysailing bowl, don't drink it in haste.

6. Come butler, come butler, give us a bowl of the best,
Hoping your soul in heaven may rest.
In heaven may rest where we shall all be.
To my waysailing bowl, we'll drink unto thee.

7. But if he should fill us a bowl of the small
Down will go butler, and bowl and all
Down he shall go to the bottom of the sea
To my waysailing bowl, we'll drink unto thee.

My wife and I heard Dick Parsons sing this song in a lively lunchtime session in 1975 in what was then a rustic pub on the edge of Cheltenham. It was the first of several versions of the Gloucestershire wassail tune that we collected and is simpler in its structure.

The Bedmaking

1.Now me fa - ther he were such a mean old man.
Sent me off to ser___ vice when I was young, but the
miss - ter-ess and me we ne - ver could a - gree be -
cause the ma___ ster he would kiss me.

1. Now my father he were such a mean old man
Sent me off to service when I was young
But me mistress and me, we could never agree
Because the master would kiss me.

2. Then the missus her sent I upstairs to the loft
To make up a bed so neat and soft
Master followed on with a little gold pin
"Take this, Betty, for bedmaking."

3. But the missus her come upstairs in haste
Copped the master with his arm around me waist
From the top of the stairs her did him fling
"Take that, Master, for the bedmaking."

4. All through the kitchen and down through the hall
All through the parlour, among the women all
Everybody asked me wherever I had been
And they laughed when I said, "At the bedmaking."

5. Then the missus her turned out of the door
Said as her didn't like a nasty little whore
The weather being wet, and my clothes being thin
How I wished as I were back at the bedmaking.

6. Six months over, seven month past
This pretty fair maid grew thick around the waist
Her stays they 'ouldn't meet nor her pinafore pin
And her cried when her thought about the bedmaking.

7. Eight month had gone and nine month coming on
When the pretty little maiden she had a little son.
Took him to the church, and had him christened John
Then she took him back to the gay old man.

8. Then she cursed him the kitchen and down through the hall
Out through the parlour, before the women all.
"If you won't pay me, take your little son John
'Cause he cost you nothing but the bedmaking."

I had this song from Bob Arnold of Burford, Oxfordshire in 1991. Bob was well known as the actor playing Tom Forrest in the long-running radio serial, The Archers. Bob grew up in a pub in the Oxfordshire village of Asthall where he heard many songs. This one was sung regularly by an old woman in the pub.

The Devil and the Farmer's Wife

1.A far-mer was plough-ing be-neath the sun. Sing-ing Mir-and-da, mi ray - eh A

far-mer was plough-ing be-neath the sun when up from the earth the De-vil come with his

Chorus:

right leg left leg, upp-er leg un-der leg. Sing-ing Mir-and-a Mi - ray - eh.

1. A farmer was ploughing beneath the sun,
Singing Miranda, Miraye-ay,
A farmer was ploughing beneath the sun
When up from the earth the Devil come
With his right leg, left leg, upper leg, under leg
Singing Miranda Miraye-ay

2. "Is it for my son that you have come?" etc
"Oh no," said the Devil, "'tis not for your son
'Tis your wife, that son of a gun," etc

3. "Oh take her, oh take her with all of my heart, etc
I pray every day that you never do part," etc

4. And so he slung her right over his back, etc
Down the hill he went wickety-wack, etc

5. Oh when she got there, she did very well, etc
She said, "Someday, I'll be Queen of Hell," etc.

6. One little devil peeped over the spire, etc
She threw ten others right into the fire, etc.

7. Another little devil peeped over the wall, etc
Saying, "Take her back, daddy, she'll kill us all," etc.

8. The farmer was peeping through the crack, etc
He saw the old Devil come lugging her back, etc.

9. So now she'll do whatever she will, etc
If the Devil won't have her, now who in hell will, etc.

Sung to me in 1998 by the remarkable Dick Richards of New York State, who despite losing a hand in an accident, still found a way to play the guitar and fiddle and was a practising musician for many years.

The Gloucester Blinder

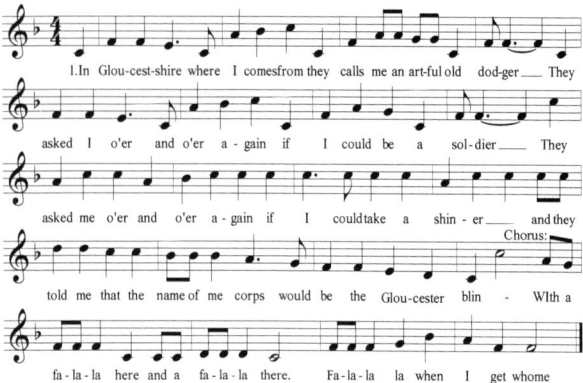

1. In Gloucestershire where I comes from, they calls
me an artful old dodger.
They asked me o'er and o'er again if I could be a
soldier
They asked me o'er and o'er again if I could take a
shiner
And they told me that the name of me corps would be
the Gloucester Blinder.

Chorus: With a fa-la-la here and a fa-la-la there.
Fa-la-la-la when I get whome.

2. They took I on the square that day, a-followin' up
the band, sir.
And a gurt tall chap way out in front, why didn't he
thump that drum, sir.
He'd swing his sticks up over his y'ead, wallop, he
brought 'em down, sir.
And he hut [hit] a gurt hole in the side of the drum, as
bigger than a mangle wurzle.

3. They took us on parade thuck [that] day, doin' our

166

duty manual
And round and round thuck square we went, as the
rifles we did handle
'Twas eyes right, eyes left, dammit hold your y'head
up
And if thee's durst as much as answer 'em back
they'd stick 'ee in the lock-up.

4. Now they brought us in 'twas dinner time, I was as
hungry as a hunter
But I dursn't touch or smell one bit, 'til the officer
had been round, sir
They brought a dish, dished it up, on an old tin platter
And all that I had when it come to my turn
Was bwone [bone] and a blooming gurt tyater
[potato].

5. Lord don't I wish I were back, a vollowin' our old
plough sir
Lord don't I wish that I were back, a-milkin' our old
cow sir
Lord don't I wish that I were back, alongside a leg o'
mutton
With a damn gurt knife and a rusty old fork, ah
lummee couldn't I cut 'en.

*David Gardner of Tresham, in the south of
Gloucestershire, gave me this song in 1997. His son,
Michael, now sings the song and has written an extra
verse in honour of his father:*

When I gets back to Gloucestershire, I'll go whome
to my village
But I could never forget thick bloody war, and the
pals lost in the carnage
I'll go to church on Sunday morn and thank the Lord

in Heaven
For the fields and the hills and the valleys and the trees
And that long old winding Severn.

The song is widely known in various versions, from Cornwall to East Anglia. This version is a good example of Gloucestershire dialect.

The Leaves of Life

1. All under the leaves and the leaves of life,
I met with virgins seven.
Foremost of them was Mary so mild,
Our Lord's dear mother in heaven.

*Variant

Lord's dear mo-ther in - Heaven.

1. All under the leaves and the leaves of life
I met with virgins seven.
Foremost of them was Mary so mild,
Our dear Lord's mother in heaven.

2. "Oh what are you seeking, you seven fair maids
All under the leaves of life?
Pray tell me, pray tell me, what seek you
All under the leaves of life?"

3. "We seek not gold nor leaves, Thomas,
For that dear son of mine
We are seeking for sweet Jesus Christ
For to be our guide and thine."

4. "Then haste ye to Jerusalem
Seek not in Galilee
For it's there you'll find sweet Jesus Christ,
Nail-ed to a gurt yew tree."

5. With haste they to Jerusalem
As fast as foot could fall.
With many a grievous bitter tear
From the virgins' eyes did fall.

6. Now when they reach-ed Calvary
The salt tears fell like rain.
"Oh, woe is me, my own dear son
For to see you bear such pain."

7. High on a cross on that green hill
With hands and feet nailed fast
Despis-ed and rejected of men
By false prophets outcast.

8. "Oh mother I pray you your weeping cease
I pray you do not grieve.
For I must suffer this," he said,
"For Adam and for Eve."

9. "Oh, how can I my weeping cease,
My sorrows overthrow?
When I do see my own son die
Sweet sons I give no more."

10. "Oh, mother sweet mother, you must take John
To be your only son
And he will comfort you betimes
Mother, as I have done."

11. "Then welcome John, the Evangelist
Then welcome unto me
More welcome yet than my own dear son
That have dangled upon my knee."

12. The rose, the rose, the blood red rose
And the fennel that grows so green.
God grant us grace in everie place
For to pray for our king and queen.

13. And furthermore for our enemies all
Our prayers they must be strong
Amen, good Lord, your sweet charity
Is the ending of my song.

Gordon Hall of Sussex was a man who took his singing very seriously and relished every syllable he sang. He told me, when he sang this song in 1996, that this song was a favourite of his family at Eastertime. His performance of it lasted eight and a half minutes.

Pompalerie Jig

1. Wellington addressed us on the eve of Waterloo
We've the Grenadier Guards and Coldstreams and you have the Scots Guards, too
And as for the old moustaches, why you shouldn't give a fig.
You've your muskets, swords and bayonets and your Pompalerie Jig.

2. And in the heat of battle on the field of Waterloo
Oh, we volleyed and we charged them and we ran them through and through
And as for the old moustaches, why, they squealed just like a pig
At our muskets, swords and bayonets and our Pompalerie Jig.

3. And at the end of battle, old Boney said, "Tell me do,
However did you beat me on the field of Waterloo?"
And we said, "We're glad you asked us for we knew you'd never twig.
It was our muskets, swords and bayonets and our Pompalerie Jig."

4. Boney sat and thought awhile and said to me, "Me man,
I think I have the answer, pray correct me if you can.
It wasn't your arms nor regiments for my armies were too big
So the only thing that defeated me was your Pompalerie Jig."

5. And how did they serve the veterans that did these daring deeds?
Why, they published us a Vagrancy Act to furnish all our needs,
All passed by act of Parliament, by the Tories and the Whigs
And they left us all with nothing but a Pompalerie Jig.

This song is satirical and unique to the singing of Ray Driscoll. No other version has been found, which is curious as it seems to date from soon after the battle of Waterloo. Ray learnt the song from an Irishman in Wigan who earned the nickname Pompey due to the frequency with which he sang the song. I recorded it from Ray in 1993. The tune is the first part of the hornpipe, Boney Crossing the Alps.

The Schoolmaster's Son

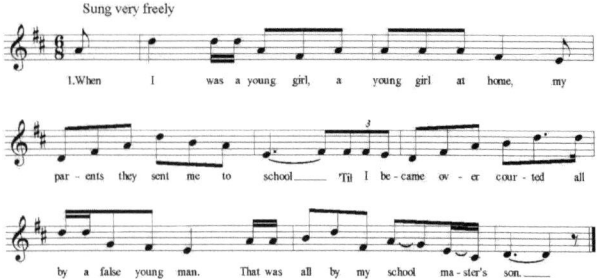

1. When I was a young girl, a young girl at home,
My parents they sent me to school,
'Til I became over-courted all by a false young man,
That was all by my schoolmaster's son.

2. Then my parents they turned me out of doors, out
of doors,
Was because my character was gone,
It never would have been if it was not for him,
That was all by my schoolmaster's son.

3. As I was a-walking up great London street,
You'd have heard of the same and before,
Who should I chance to spy but my own true love
Where my thoughts would never would have been
[sic – as sung].

4. For he tiled me an apple along of the floor,
He was thinking to 'tice me once more,
I tiled it back again, straight back to him again,
"Your apple it's rotten to the core."

5. "Come hold up your head pretty maid, pretty maid,
Come hold up your head, don't cry dear,
We'll have wedding bells to ring, we'll have college
girls to sing,
We'll have tied hands all on our wedding day."

This song is rare indeed. A version was collected, again from a Gypsy in Gloucestershire in 1921. Gwilym recorded Danny Brazil singing this version in Gloucestershire in 1978, which is the only time it has been recorded in oral tradition.

The Shooting Gallery

1. It's through a shooting gallery I'm settled now for life,
For there I first beheld the girl I since have made my wife.
She held a rifle in her hand in such a winning way
And when I took it from her, she smilingly did say

Chorus: "You've got to hit the bull's-eye before you ring the bell
Take a steady aim, love, and try to do it well.
Hold your rifle higher and don't let it misfire
For you've got to hit the bull's-eye before you ring the bell.

2. I quickly fired the rifle but I failed to ring the bell
Although I tried, it was no use, how 'twas I cannot tell.
I did as she instructed me, and for a shot paid her.
In such a coaxing manner, she whispered in my ear.

3. I kept on firing but I found the bull's-eye far too small.
The more I kept on firing, it was never hit at all.
And then she said, "Try one more shot, for really you can't tell.
The next time that you fire your gun, perhaps you'll ring the bell."

4. And now to tell the truth, my friends, and cut my story short,
I'm married now and I'm now at home and got some proper sport
I've got a shooting gallery in a garret near the sky
When I look out of my window, all my neighbours quickly cry.

This cheeky song is older than it looks and can be traced back to a 19ᵗʰ century broadside. It is very rare in tradition, but Arthur Baker of North Warnborough, Hampshire, sang it to me with a wide grin in 1972.

The Streets of Minturno

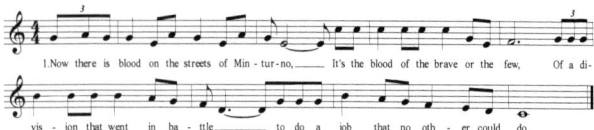

1.Now there is blood on the streets of Min - tur-no,_____ It's the blood of the brave or the few, Of a di-

vis - ion that went in ba - ttle_____ to do a job that no oth - er could do.

1. Now there is blood on the streets of Minturno
It's the blood of the brave or the few.
Of a division that went into battle
To do a job that no other could do.

2. Now the Yanks said they couldn't cross that river
They said it just couldn't be done
And to prove what they thought of our chances
They were betting at twenty to one.

3. But they didn't know the old Fifth Division
When there's a job to be done
There was nothing on earth what could stop us
Not even the square-headed Hun.

4. So forward we went into battle
Not a man thought of death.
All grim and looking determined
But in their hearts they were saying a prayer.

5. Yes, they thought of their wives, their mothers
They thought of the loved ones who knew
For they knew when they crossed over the river
There was many who'd never return.

6. Yes there's blood on the streets of Minturno.
It's the blood of the brave and the few.
May their souls live in glory forever
And their hearts live in heaven above.

The Italian town of Minturno was the scene in 1944 of a battle involving British, American and German troops. The song suggests that the British forces were able to succeed where the American forces had not. This unique song was sung to me by Don Mitchell of Stroud on 28 October 1979.

The White Cockade

1. 'Tis true my love's enlisted, he wears the white cockade.
He is both gay and handsome as any roving blade.
He's gone to be a soldier, the white cockade he wears,
While I am here awaiting in sorrow and despair.

2. "Leave off your grief and sorrow, likewise your doleful strain.
The white cockade adorns me as I march o'er the plain.
When I return, I'll marry by this cockade I'll swear.
'Til then, my love, be patient and my departure bear."

3. "I bring to you sad tidings," the sergeant he did say.
"Your love was slain in battle, he sends you this today."
He handed her the plumage, bedraggled by his gore.
"With his last kiss he sent it, the white cockade he wore."

4. She spoke no words and at her tears, they fell in salten flood,
And from the bedraggled plumage she washed the stains of blood.
"Oh mother, I am dying, and when I'm in my grave
Just pin it to my bosom, my lover's white cockade."

This song, The White Cockade, is known to many people in the folk song revival but most versions stop at the soldier going off to war with a promise to return and marry his sweetheart. Charlie Hill's version is unusual, having the soldier die on the battlefield and his lover dying of grief, but a similar version was collected in Devon by the Rev Baring-Gould. Charlie learnt his version from Gypsy singers in Devon and sang it to me in 1985.

Wild, Wild Berry

1. Young man came from hunting faint and weary.
"What does ail my lord, my dearie?"
"Oh mother dear, let my bed be made
For I fear the gripe of the woody nightshade."
Lie low, sweet Randal,

Chorus: So come all you young men that do eat full well
And they that sup right merry
'Tis far better, I entreat to have toads for your meat
Than to eat of the wild, wild berry.

2. Now this young man he died eft soon
All by the light of the hunter's moon.
'Twas not by bolt nor yet by blade
But the deadly gripe of the woody nightshade.
Lie low, sweet Randal

3. This lord's false love they hanged her high
For her deeds were the cause of ther love to die
And in her hair they entwined a braid
Of the leaves and berries of the woody nightshade.
Lie low, sweet Randal.

This curious song was sung to me many times by Ray Driscoll, who learnt it from a farm worker in Shropshire. It seems to be a reworking of the Lord Randal ballad, but no other version of Wild, Wild Berry has come to light.

There was a Lady gay

1. There was a lady gay and in our town did dwell
She loved her husband dearlye and another one twice
as well.

Chorus: Mush-em tiggery awri awri
Mush-em tiggery awri-ay

2. She listened at the keyhole, she heard the old man
say
"If I suck six dozen marrybones it'll take my sight
away."

3. She ran to the butcher to see what she could find
She got six dozen marrybones to make the old man
blind.

4. She took them to the old man; she made him suck
them all
"Now," said the old man, "I cannot see at all."

5. "It's you that's sick and blind," said she, "and here
you cannot stay
But if you'd like to drown yourself, I'll gladly lead
the way."

6. She took him gently by the hand and led him to a stream
"You'll have to help me," said the old man, "I cannot see a thing."

7. She got upon the brink to push the old man in.
He stuck out his feet and she went thrashing in.

8. "It's murder, it's murder," as loud as could scream
"I'd help you, "said the old man, "but I cannot see a thing."

9. He being kind-hearted, he knew she couldn't swim
He went and got a long pole and pushed her further in.

10. "I have eleven children and none of them are mine.
I wish that every country gent would come and claim his own."

This is a version of the song universally known as Marrowbones or The Blind Man He Could See. Phyllis Marks of West Virginia, herself blind, sang it for me in 1998. The last verse is unusual and perhaps comes from another song. It is easy to understand why the man should want to get rid of his wife if she has had eleven children from other fathers!

Three Brothers in Fair Warwickshire

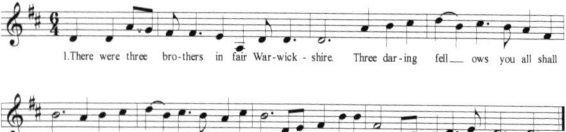

1.There were three bro-thers in fair War-wick - shire. Three dar-ing fell___ ows you all shall hear. To rob and plu___nder was their in - tent. to go robb-ing a - long the high___ way they went. ___

1. There were three brothers fair in Warwickshire
Three daring young men you all shall hear.
To rob and plunder was their intent
To go robbing along the highway they went.

2. The first they met it was Lord Grangeville
With his coach and four there they did rebay,
The heavy blow struck him on the head
And they left him on the highway for dead.

3. They took his watch and his money too
So soon they prov-ed his sad overthrow,
They run away it's with all their speed
And they left him on the highway to bleed..

4. Now they were taken all for the same
They was put in prison 'til the trial came.
They was put in prison bound in iron strong
Until the 'sizes it did come on.

5. Now at the bar these three young men 'peared
They was pleading guilty you all shall hear,
The judge and jurymen all did say
For those are cast and condemned today.

6. "Their names, their names have you young men three?
Your names your names you come to tell me,"
"My name's Will Atkins, from whence I came."
"Yes, and many a time I have heard your name."

7. "Their age, their age have you young men three?
Your age, your age you come to tell me."
"One eighteen, nineteen and the other twenty
[repeat tune of previous line] Isn't it a shocking and a sight to see
Three clever young men on the gallows tree?"

8. Now at the bar their poor mother 'peared
She was a -wringing of her tender hands, tearing out her hair
Saying, "Judge and jurymen, spare their lives
For they are my sons and my heart's delight."

9. "It's go you home, dearest woman, dear,
You've come too late, for their time it's near.
Tomorrow morning at the hour of three
You can claim their bodies from the gallows tree."

10. "It's go you home, dearest mother, dear,
You've come too late, for our time it's near.
Tomorrow morning, that is the day
And from all our friends we must die away."

11. "Come all you people that is standing by
That have come here for to see us die
You shun bad company, take to good ways
That's the way to live and see happy days."

This sombre and rare ballad was remembered by the Gypsy, Danny Brazil, from Staverton, Gloucestershire, and sung to me in 1978. Gallows ballads and last confessions were popular broadside material and this refers to a true incident which took place in 1818.

Three Little Babes

1. There was a bride, a most beautiful bride
Three little babes had she
She sent them away to a northern college
To learn their grammaree.

2. They hadn't been away but a little while
'Bout three months and a day
'Til death spread wide all over the land
And took her babes away.

3. "Oh, Saviour dear," cried the beautiful bride
Who used to wear a crown
"Send to me my three little babes
Tonight or in the morning soon."

4. But it being close to Christmas time
And the nights being long and cold
Down come running those three little babes
Into their mother's home.

5. She fixed them a table in the backside room
Spread over with bread and wine
"Come and eat and drink, my three little babes
Come and eat and drink of mine."

6. "We can't eat your bread, sweet mother dear
Neither can we drink your wine
For yonder stands my sweet Saviour
From this we must resign."

7. She fixed them a bed in the backside room
Spread over with a nice clean sheet
On top of that was a golden spread
She fixed them a place to sleep.

8. "Take it off, take it off, sweet mother dear
Take it off," then again said he
"How can we stay in this wide wicked world
When there's a better place for me."

*In the autumn of 1997, I travelled down to Chilhowie,
Virginia, to meet and record 79 year old Spencer Moore
in his modest cabin. He had already been visited by
several song collectors, including Alan Lomax and
Shirley Collins in the fifties. This song was the gem of
his repertoire and derives from the old British ballad of
The Wife Of Usher's Wife, long forgotten in the British
Isles but still in oral tradition in the Appalachians.*

Three Men Went a-Hunting

1. For it's three men went a-hunting to see what they could find.
Until they came to a hedgehog and that they left behind.
The Englishman said it was a hedgehog, the Scotsman he said, "Nay."
And Paddy said 'twas a pincushion with the pins turned the 'tother way.

Chorus [to same tune]: For 'twas half past five in the morning in the middle of the night.
The ducks began to quarrel and the pigs began to fight.
The neighbours looked out of the window to see that all was right,
For 'twas half past five in the morning in the middle of the night.

2. For it's three men went a-hunting to see what they could find.
Until they came to a donkey and that they left behind.
The Englishman said it was a donkey, the Scotsman he said, "Nay."
And Paddy said 'twas his grandfather with his hair all growing grey.

3. For it's three men went a-hunting to see what they could find.
Until they came to a cowpat and that they left behind.
The Englishman said it was a cowpat, the Scotsman he said, "Nay."
And Paddy said 'twas a rhubarb tart with the crust all blowed away.

4. For it's three men went a-hunting to see what they could find.
Until they came to a haystack and that they left behind.
The Englishman said it was a haystack, the Scotsman he said, "Nay."
And Paddy said 'twas an old thatched barn with its windows blowed away.

The gentle humour of this song has persisted in English tradition for nearly five hundred years. My wife and I collected it from George Privett of Shedfield, Hampshire, in 1974.

Wassail Song (Woodchester)

1. Waysail, waysail, all over the town,
Our bread it is white and our ale it is brown.
And our bowl it is made of the best mottling tree,
To the waysailing bowl I'll bring unto thee.

2. Now here's a health to our master and to his right
eye,
Pray God send our master a good Xmas [sic] pie,
And a good Xmas pie that we may all see
To me waysailing bowl I'll bring unto thee.

3. Now here's a health to our master and to his right
ear
Pray God send our master a happy New Year.
And a happy New Year that we may all see
To me waysailing bowl I'll bring unto thee.

4. Now here's a health to my master and to his right
arm,
Pray God send our master a good crop of corn,
And a good crop of corn and another of hay
To pass the cold wintery wyunds (winds) away.

5. Now here's a health to my master and to his right hip,
Pray God send our master a good flock of ship (sheep),
And a good flock of ship that we may all see;
To me waysailing bowl I'll bring unto thee.

6. Now here's a health to my master and to his right leg,
Pray God send our master a good fatted pig.
And a good fatted pig that we may all see
To me waysailing bowl I'll bring unto thee.

7. Now butler come fill us a bowl of your best
I hope that in Heaven your soul will rest
But if you should bring us a bowl of your small
Then down shall go butler, bowl and all.

8. There was an old woman she had but one cow
And how to maintain it she did not know how
She built up a barn to keep her cow warm
And a drop of your cider will do us no harm.

This splendid version of the Gloucestershire wassail was sung to us by Billy Buckingham of Stonehouse, Gloucestershire, in 1997. He had learnt it as a lad in the Stroud area and used to earn money (and cider!) by singing it around the big houses and farms at Christmas time in the area south of Stroud, down to Woodchester.

Index

Songs and Tunes